Coming Back

Coming Back

The Community Experiences of Deinstitutionalized Mentally Retarded People

Elinor Gollay
Ruth Freedman
Marty Wyngaarden
Norman R. Kurtz

Abt Books
Cambridge, Massachusetts

Library of Congress Catalog Card Number 78-68165

© Abt Associates Inc., 1978

Printed in the United States of America.

ISBN: 0-89011-512-5

This book is dedicated to the over 400 mentally retarded people and their families who gave generously of their time to be interviewed. Their hopes as well as those of the authors were stated simply and eloquently by one of the study group members, who added the following at the end of his interview: "I wish this will help someone else."

Table of Contents

Tables

Appendices

Preface

This book brings to the reader a new and important aspect of mental retardation as a social phenomenon. It documents in engaging detail how those traditionally referred to as mentally retarded are steadily advancing toward a more meaningful participation in society, while those who caused them to be known as retarded continue to reflect a "retarded" prejudicial perception.

Another significant contribution of this book is its realistic and reassuring yet challenging assessment of the state of the art in community placement of persons with mental retardation. With relevant data drawn from a nationally significant sample, the authors show that community residences even at this early stage do a far more adequate job than citizens and the families with mentally retarded children have been led to believe by newspaper accounts and specific attacks against "deinstitutionalization" which, if carefully read, in most cases refer to persons released from hospitals for the mentally ill.

While the study of course points to areas where programs in the community residences need improvement (the authors wisely have excluded nursing homes as providing a different type of care), the primary and most serious deficiencies are found in the area of pre-placement training, and in the glaring lack of supportive community services, particularly the lack of opportunities for employment or meaningful occupation for adults.

The quality of the study was considerably enhanced by the decision to include the mentally retarded persons among those interviewed. The results showed that this was a sound, indeed an essential step — they were able to speak for themselves quite pointedly and their reactions to their move from the institution to the community residence make the study's findings all the more meaningful.

Within the confines of this study the authors were unable to deal with one aspect which is of crucial significance, the role and function of the state agencies ultimately responsible for these publicly supported programs. At least in some states the trend appears to be to put too broad a burden on the private "vendor" providing the residence, while the responsible department has a maze of stifling rules, regulations, guidelines and directives — a poor substitute for diligence on the part of the public agency in direct monitoring of the well-being of individual clients.

It is not hard to foresee that this misplaced bureaucratic preoccupation will increasingly conflict with what this study documents most poignantly: the emergence of the persons with mental retardation into society with a far greater capacity for a meaningful human existence, a far keener sense of their own needs and limitations and a much more distinct striving for a better life than is expected even today by those charged with planning for their welfare.

Rosemary and Gunnar Dybwad

Acknowledgments

The study upon which this book is based was conducted by Abt Associates Inc. under contract to the Bureau of Education for the Handicapped, United States Office of Education (Contract No. OEC 0-74-9183). Without the efforts of the people who participated in that study this book would not have been possible. Those who contributed to the conduct of the study were the field interviewers, the retarded people hired to help train these interviewers, many staff at Abt Associates Inc. who assisted in designing the study, coding and analyzing the data, and individuals in the research division of BEH.

There were also many people who made the book itself possible. Joe Clark carried out the necessary computer runs for the additional analyses performed. Special thanks go to the many people who helped type various drafts of the manuscript, especially Ina Moses, Harriet Merriman, and Marcia Knopf. We also wish to thank copy editor Tory Alexander for her expert assistance and the Abt Associates Publications staff.

Most important, this book would not have been possible without the unstinting contributions of the retarded people and their families who were interviewed and the staff of the participating institutions who contributed many hours to ensure that the project was carried out successfully. Rarely did any of these participants deviate from the aim of providing us with a true picture of the prerelease and postrelease experiences of deinstitutionalized mentally retarded persons. The authors sincerely hope that this book adequately reflects the dedication and concern which we found "in the field" with the people who daily are living with the realities of coming back into the community.

E.G.
R.F.
M.W.
N.K.

May 1978

Chapter I
Introduction

Mentally retarded people have been released in increasing numbers from the nation's institutions. What are their experiences in "the community"? Where are they living? What are they doing during the day? How are they spending their leisure time? Do they have friends? Are they receiving the services and training which they need? How do they feel about their experiences in the community? Why do some people return to the institution?

These are some of the questions we address in this book. The information we present does not provide conclusive answers. Rather, the picture which emerges most clearly is one of diversity: mentally retarded people enter the community with differing personal characteristics and experiences. Some are virtually "normal" except for their institutional experiences. Others are multiply handicapped by a combination of physical and mental limitations; some have visible facial or other deformities while others have none.

Institutionalized retarded people live in various kinds of environments; some provide intensive training while others offer few supports. The diversity continues in the community. The retarded people interviewed in this study were placed in community settings which range from isolated homes with few amenities to houses offering many services; from remote rural communities to crowded urban settings. Similarly, the people engaged in a variety of school, work, and spare-time activities. Some participated in many activities and had several friends, too many others engaged in few activities and had few social contacts.

Overall, the retarded people whose community experiences are described in this book had positive experiences in the community: they perceived themselves and were perceived by their "families" as adjusting well to life in the community. They were glad to be in the community rather than in the institution and were anxious to learn how to be better members of the community. Within the generally positive picture which emerged, there were also many problems or difficulties which the people faced. The chapters which follow provide more detailed information about the diversity — and the positive and negative aspects — of these community experiences.

DESCRIPTION OF THE STUDY

The information presented in the book is based upon a study which was conducted from 1974 to 1976. Our main purpose was to assess the community experiences of deinstitutionalized mentally retarded people and to identify the factors related to their experiences. We wished to obtain a broad picture of their residential settings, day activities (work or school), leisure activities, and service and training needs. In attempting to understand better the factors which might influence the community experiences of the study group members, we also sought information on the characteristics of the releasing institutions, the experiences which the individuals had at these institutions, the characteristics of the residences to which they were released, and the individual characteristics of the study group members themselves. By looking at the variety of community experiences, institutional backgrounds, and individual characteristics, we hoped to shed some light on the enormously complex process known as "community adjustment."

The project entailed a number of steps, which are described in detail in Appendix A and briefly outlined here. First, we contacted over 250 public and private institutions throughout the country to determine how many individuals had been released to the community between 1972 and 1974. Over 150 institutions responded to the initial survey, and nine of these were subsequently selected for participation in the study. We visited the nine institutions to obtain more detailed information, particularly in regard to their prerelease programs. The institutions compiled mailing lists of all the individuals between the ages of 6 and 40 who were released into community settings during the specified time period. Letters and consent forms were sent to these persons seeking their participation in the study. Only those who had lived in the institution for at least two years prior to their release were included.

In addition, only individuals placed in community settings rather than in other institutions were asked to participate. Community settings consisted of a variety of placements, including natural families, foster families, group homes, semi-independent living arrangements, and independent living arrangements. Specifically excluded were residential settings which were highly restrictive, had more than 100 residents, or were considered nursing homes. In fact, none of the members of the study group lived in facilities with more than 25 residents.

The final study group consisted of the 440 people who agreed to participate. Of these, 382 (87 percent) were still living in the community when interviewed in the summer of 1975, and the remaining 58 (13 percent) had returned to live in an institution.

The interviews were conducted with both the mentally retarded people and their "families." "Families" is used throughout the book to refer to the people with whom the study group members were living at the time of the interviews (or in the case of those who returned to institutions, immediately prior to readmission). Families included natural parents, foster parents, group home staff, and personnel overseeing semi-independent living situations. In the case of people living independently, a "significant other person," generally a social worker or employer, was interviewed in place of the family.

The interviewers found virtually all of the people they interviewed — families and retarded people alike — cooperative and interested in the study. Sometimes it was difficult for retarded people to understand certain items and concepts which were used but, in general, they appeared eager to be helpful and accurate as respondents.

Precautions were taken in order to protect the privacy of the mentally retarded persons. We sent carefully designed consent forms to prospective participants and only those agreeing to participate were contacted. In the chapters which follow, information is presented only in aggregated form so that individuals cannot be identified; none of the information obtained about or from individuals was given to anyone else (i.e., institutional or community agency personnel).

UNDERLYING PRINCIPLES

We were influenced by a number of principles or themes in designing and conducting this study; the most important are listed here.

The views of mentally retarded individuals about what and how they are doing in the community are extremely important. Every effort should therefore be made by researchers (policymakers, planners, providers, and so forth) to solicit and incorporate their views. As a result of this principle, special questionnaires were designed which were administered directly to the mentally retarded persons, without family members present. Interviewers were hired because of their experience in dealing with retarded individuals and were given extensive training in administering the questionnaires. In addition, mentally retarded individuals were hired as consultants to assist in training the interviewers.

The concept of "community adjustment" is not one-dimensional, but rather reflects multiple aspects of living and coping in the community. A strong theme throughout the project was that of examining many aspects of a mentally retarded person's life — his or her residence, daily activities, and social life. We made no attempt to "measure" the adjustment of retarded persons, but instead reviewed their accomplishments and experiences in a number of important areas.

Behavioral standards for judging mentally retarded people should not be different from or harsher than those against which nonretarded persons are judged. Many existing scales for measuring the performance of retarded persons include specific evaluations of behavior which would not be applied to the behavior of nonretarded people. At another level, we tried to keep in mind that the question of how one is "doing" in the community varies greatly from person to person and from one period of time to another.

How well a retarded person adjusts to the community is likely to be a complex function of characteristics of the individual, his or her previous experiences and training, the institution from which he or she was released, and the community into which he or she is released. Traditionally, studies of the community adjustment of retarded people focus on the characteristics of the individual — IQ, psychological characteristics, age, sex, and so on. While these are no doubt important, we felt that it was even more important to examine the environmental factors. The policy implications of such factors are crucial: examination of individual characteristics can lead to statements about who should and should not be released to the community; examination of environmental factors tells us what can be altered in the prelease or postrelease environment to help the individual adapt successfully to the community. Thus, we investigated external factors, as well as individual characteristics, in the hope that this focus would help shift the burden of responsibility for success or failure from the individual to the community.

ORGANIZATION OF THE BOOK

The book is organized into 11 chapters, including this introduction. Throughout the chapters describing the community experiences of retarded people, information is reported in terms of the total study group, differences between children and adults, and differences among three levels of retardation (mild, moderate, and severe/profound).

Chapter II provides an historical overview of the context in which the study took place. It was the quality of past information which set the stage for the entire study, prompting us to formulate the principles just described and seek particular kinds of information.

Chapter III reports data from families and institutional records on the study group members, including age, level of retardation, additional disabilities, history of institutionalization, and participation in institutional programs. Our purpose is to provide a sketch of the attributes which individuals brought into the community — a combination of individual characteristics and experiences gained prior to release.

Chapter IV presents extensive information on the characteristics of the homes in which study group members were living at the time of the interviews, the characteristics of the families, the study group members' residential histories, and satisfaction with the setting.

Chapter V describes the daily activities of the study group members at the time of the study (work, school, day activity centers), the history of their daily activities, and their satisfaction with and success in current activities.

Chapter VI presents information on friendships, social activities within the home, and spare-time activities. These data were obtained primarily from the families. Also included are observations on loneliness, romantic relationships, and ability to get along with others — information provided by both families and the retarded people.

Chapter VII describes the services received in the community. Families were asked to indicate the services both they and study group members were using, who was providing the services, and the frequency of use. We also note situations in which services were needed but not used. Included in the category of services are various personal supports: institutional follow-up, involvement of community case managers, and the presence of another individual who could provide support.

Chapter VIII presents information on community-based training. As with services, families were asked to indicate which types of training study group members used, who provided the training, and how frequently. We also report instances in which training was needed, and those in which training was not needed because the individual either already had the skill or was not yet ready to learn it.

Cutting across each of the major areas described above (residential setting, activities, social contacts, services and training), Chapter IX describes the various problems people were having in the community. In addition, the chapter explores the reasons why some individuals were returned to an institution.

Chapter X describes those people who have subsequently returned to an institution. Focusing on individual characteristics and community experiences, we describe the major differences between those who returned to the institution and those who remained in the community. Highlighted are differences in behavior problems, participation in community activities, utilization of institutional resources, and overall satisfaction and adjustment.

Chapter XI presents a brief overview of the experiences of mentally retarded people and their families, again cutting across the specific aspects presented in earlier chapters.

Appendices A through K present a number of supplementary materials for the interested reader: a more detailed description of the study methodology and tables which shed additional light on the differences between children and adults or among the three levels of retardation. Where appropriate in the following chapters, references are made to specific tables in the appendices which provide additional data from the interviews.

Chapter II
The Historical Context

The transition of mentally retarded persons from institutional to community living — the process of deinstitutionalization — is perhaps best understood in its historical context. Only about 130 years ago it was thought that institutional settings could provide the best environment for mentally retarded persons, and in the years which followed increasing numbers of mentally retarded people were moved from their homes to institutions. Why were they moved to institutions in the first place? What values and attitudes did this treatment reflect?

Recent trends have reversed the process and increased the likelihood that individuals of all ages and at all levels of retardation will live in communities. Many people now living in communities previously lived in institutions, some for substantial portions of their lives. Why are they now *coming back* to establish homes in the community?

This chapter reviews some of the important historical patterns in the treatment of mentally retarded people and explores the attitudes and values behind these social trends. This historical approach provides insight into the new perspective on mentally retarded people — a perspective based on the assumption that such individuals have a right to participate to the fullest possible extent in the life of the "normal" community.

AN HISTORICAL OVERVIEW OF INSTITUTIONALIZATION

Mentally retarded people, along with many of society's "misfits," were placed in training facilities beginning primarily around the middle of the nineteenth century. At the time, the emphasis was on training and preparing "poor unfortunates" for eventual return to society as stable, productive members.

> All these early schools for the retarded were organized in the hope of largely overcoming, if not entirely curing, mental retardation by the application of the physiological method, and of so greatly improving the condition of patients that they could be returned to the community, capable of self-guidance and of earning an independent livelihood. These schools were, therefore, frankly educational institutions.[1]

Institutions for all types of "deviants" were being established in the mid-1800's by socially concerned reformers. Wolfensberger argues that this educational orientation was part of the desire of the reformers to tackle the problem of deviance in society by, in effect, trying to cure it:

> Around 1850, institutions for a number of deviant groups in the United States were founded for the purpose of making the deviant less deviant. The main means whereby this was to be accomplished was education. In effect, the argument was that deviants have to be congregated in one place so that expert and intensive attention could be concentrated on them.[2]

This movement, then, not only affected mentally retarded persons, but was part of a general trend which included the establishment of almshouses for poor people, penal institutions for criminals, and insane asylums for mentally ill people. David Rothman's comprehensive historical study of the growth of institutions in the United States does not include institutions for mentally retarded persons, but the overall trend seems clear:

> The reaction to the problem of dependency (i.e., poverty) paralleled the response to the issue of deviancy. Just as the penitentiary would reform the criminal and the insane asylum would cure the mentally ill, so the almshouse would rehabilitate the poor.[3]

Thus, institutions were established as part of a reform movement aimed at bettering the lives of mentally retarded, poor, mentally ill, and other deviant people.

The institutions, first known as training schools, gradually grew larger as communities found it convenient to place elsewhere those citizens who were most difficult to handle or who were least able to contribute to the economy. Many factors contributed to the growth of these institutions and to their gradual shift from educational facilities intended to return their charges to the community "cured" of their deviancy, to residential facilities where people were committed for life. One reason for the growth and the shift in purpose was articulated by Stanley Davies in the 1950's; his perspective mirrored professional beliefs at the time:

> Gradually, however, it became clear that severe retardation was not curable or even greatly improvable . . . . The children admitted for training, while not curable as regards their intellectual defect, were teachable and they profited by the physiological method to the extent of their limited endowments. The improvement shown, however, was frankly not nearly so great as had been originally anticipated. Only a very small proportion of the pupils could be returned to the community, even after years of training, on a self-supporting basis. This changed the aspect of the whole problem. It created an unforeseen difficulty. It had not been intended, when these schools were organized, that the state should assume indefinite custodial care of these cases. The state was simply to educate them by a special method during the regular school period . . . . It became more and more evident that the state must squarely face the large and less hopeful problem of providing indefinite custodial care for a growing number of cases. So the idea of the institution as an educational project pure and simple had to be abandoned. More and more it was recognized that the state would have to enlarge its institutional accommodations to make provisions for thousands of the retarded.[4]

Wolf Wolfensberger identifies three major uses of the large institutions for mentally retarded persons: the first, which has been discussed, was to cure the deviant; the second was to protect the deviant from the nondeviant; and the third was to protect the nondeviant from the deviant.[5] Both the second and the third uses of the institution resulted in the same policy: keep the two groups separated, and in particular remove deviants from the mainstream of society. In many ways the use of the institution described by Davies corresponds to the second use noted by Wolfensberger: taking care of people assumed to be permanently deviant who would not be able to function effectively in society and who, therefore, for their own sake, should be removed from it. The third use of institutions identified by Wolfensberger existed earlier in the form of penitentiaries and, perhaps, insane asylums. Davies summarizes the transition from the first to the third use of institutions for mentally retarded people in a discussion of the growth of the eugenics movement:

> The findings of the hereditary character, the rapid multiplication, and the wide prevalence of mental deficiency were of special moment in the light of the supposed social shortcomings of the mentally handicapped. Prior to the opening of the twentieth century when mental defectives were thought of in terms of the lower-grade classes, the question of the antisocial conduct of the mentally deficient had scarce-

ly received any attention. The irresponsibility of certain types was apparent, to be sure, but the ready recognition of the severely retarded and the comparatively small number of such cases facilitated the necessary custodial care and supervision . . . . [However] *what was regarded in 1877 as primarily a problem of criminal degeneracy, became in 1915 primarily a problem of mental deficiency.* (emphasis added.)[6]

Mentally retarded people were seen as the root of many of society's evils. Wolfensberger quotes a number of the most outspoken proponents of the theory that mental retardation — or, as it was called in those days, "feeblemindedness" — was the cause of all of society's evils:

Of all dependent classes there are none that drain so entirely the social and financial life of the body politic as the imbecile, unless it be its close associate, the epileptic . . . . Feeblemindedness produces more pauperism, degeneracy and crime than any other one force . . . .[7]

Thus, many of the institutions for mentally retarded people, which had originally been established as a humane way of preparing them to live in the community, became warehouses storing those people deemed by society to be harmful to it. Commitment had originally been viewed as temporary; it gradually became permanent.

Beginning in the 1920's, another philosophical shift took place. Mentally retarded people were no longer regarded as necessarily evil; and commitment to institutions was considered appropriate mainly for the severely retarded, for whom only good custodial care was thought to be possible.

Emphasis was frequently placed on protecting the family from the overwhelming burden and disruptive influence of having a handicapped child. Parents were told that the best solution for them was to place their child in an institution as soon as possible, and then to forget that they ever had the child. Again, the objective was to provide the best custodial care possible. The purpose of the institutions, according to this perspective, was threefold: meet the basic life needs of a mentally retarded person, shelter that person from the demands of a competitive society, and relieve society of the burden of dealing with the mentally retarded individual.

This philosophy persisted until the 1950's, and is reflected in the description by Davies of "modern trends":

The institution is an essential part of a total program for the mentally deficient. It provides for many who cannot be advantageously cared for in the community. By continuous study and observation, it learns the potential for community life of all who come to its doors . . . . In the years approaching the mid-century a number of new trends can be observed . . . . A growing national trend is to admit to institutions children under five or six years of age. Young retarded children, especially if infirm, are sometimes a crushing burden in the home, but in the past institutions seldom accepted them, except in emergencies . . . Another trend is that institutions are steadily moving toward the community. The isolation that once characterized them is fast disappearing . . . .[8]

Beginning in the 1950's, it was discovered that, in many cases, mentally retarded people could learn to do things which it had been previously assumed they were incapable of learning. Parents of mentally retarded children began to talk openly about their children and demand greater support for them — both within the community and within the institution. Parents also found that the state systems were not willing to provide institutionalization. Community care, as an alternative to the institution, was increasingly seen as desirable, particularly for more "capable" mentally retarded people. Because public schools were usually unwilling to admit all but mildly retarded children, parents banded together to form their own programs, based upon the growing belief that in fact something could be done for mentally retarded people. Nursery schools, day programs, and workshops began to proliferate throughout the country, gradually receiving state or federal funding; in many instances, these programs were even taken over by the respective states.

However, such programs left unresolved the issue of where mentally retarded people should live. With few exceptions, there were only two alternatives until the mid-1960's: the parents' home and the institution. Many of the parents who had been active in forming parents' associations and various day programs had become active in these endeavors shortly after their own mentally retarded children were born. Thus, the first programs created were nursery schools. As participants in these programs grew older, sheltered workshops were established for them and for other teenagers and young adults. Many parents of older mentally retarded children joined in establishing the workshops. But where would these children live when they reached adulthood or when their parents died? Group homes were formed in response to these concerns.

Paralleling these efforts to establish new programs for mentally retarded people already living in the community, a similar trend began to grow within the institutions. Program planners, social philosophers, and direct care staff were increasingly concerned with finding ways in which mentally retarded people could realize their potential. Many of the people who had been institutionalized during the 1920's, 1930's, and 1940's — some of whom were immigrants or children of immigrants — had been committed because of poverty, epilepsy, or lack of family support. The staff at the institutions were beginning to realize that these people were not retarded but simply deprived of adequate learning opportunities. As a result of this new awareness, many individuals were released from institutions during the 1960's, often with a minimum of structured support.

By the end of the decade there had been a number of exposes of conditions in the state institutions for mentally retarded people, and state officials were being pressured to provide alternatives. The states began to fund the establishment of group homes or community residences for mentally retarded people. This was part of a larger trend in human services and paralleled, for example, the formation of "halfway houses" for mentally ill people. These facilities were intended to help bridge the gap between institutional, life and independent existence. Gradually, throughout the 1970's, more types of community residences for mentally retarded people were conceived and established.

Trends and philosophies overlap, and certain beliefs which have previously been rejected often come back into fashion. What Davies in the 1950's considered a positive trend toward increased institutional care of children, is usually seen in the 1970's as undesirable. Many state institutions no longer admit children under six except in the case of an emergency. In fact, a growing number of people now argue that there is no future role for the large-scale isolated institution as it has existed for over 100 years in this country. One of the principal advocates of this position is Wolfensberger. In his book, *The Principle of Normalization in Human Services*, Wolfensberger argues that institutional care should be avoided, in favor of the "utilization of means which are as culturally normative as possible, in order to establish and/ or maintain personal behaviors and characteristics which are as culturally normative as possible."[9] The specific implications of this principle in terms of institutions are clear:

> I can see no reason why small, specialized living units (mostly hostels) cannot accommodate almost all of the persons now in institutions. In turn, I believe that many persons who could be well served in hostels will be served even better in individual placement. Thus, we should bring about not only movement from institutions to other group residences, but also a decline in the demand for any type of group residence . . . . In sum, there are many features associated with a normalized residential model which will tend to diminish the need for residential places of any kind.[10]

DEINSTITUTIONALIZATION: FACTS AND FINDINGS

The increased trend toward serving mentally retarded people in the community has affected both institutions and the mentally retarded people in them. One of the primary effects has been a dramatic increase in the number of mentally retarded people released from institutions to community-based residences. Frequently, the process of deinstitutionalization has simply meant release of an individual from an institution; from the perspective of the institution, it has meant a decrease in the inpatient census. In 1970 President Nixon set a national goal that within ten years the population in the nation's institutions for mentally retarded persons would be halved.

The year 1967 was pivotal in the history of mentally retarded people; this was the first year in which the number of institutionalized mentally retarded individuals began to decline. Initially, the decline was gradual, showing a decrease of only 8 percent from 1967 to 1971.[11] Then it accelerated considerably; from 1971 to 1974 the institutionalized population was reduced by 25 percent.[12]

Figure II.1 shows the average daily resident population of 237 public institutions for five fiscal years, from 1971 through 1976. The reduction in population from 181,035 in fiscal year 1971-72 to 153,584 in fiscal year 1975-76 represents a 15 percent decrease. There was an 8 percent decrease from 1971-72 to 1973-74, the period approximately corresponding to the years during which the mentally retarded individuals whom we interviewed were released. For those who are committed to the principle of normalization (" . . . making available to all mentally retarded people patterns of life and conditions of everyday living which are as close as possible to the regular circumstances and ways of life in society"[13]) these statistics are encouraging.

Several attempts have been made to evaluate the impact of deinstitutionalization, particularly in terms of its effects on the mentally retarded people involved in the process. It is difficult to generalize about these studies, both because the trend is new and because of the difficulties inherent in studies of the intensely personal and unique experiences of deinstitutionalized persons. Nevertheless, a brief review of past studies provides some important insights.

One effort to make general conclusions based on the findings of a large number of studies was made by McCarver and Craig in 1974.[14] They attempted to integrate the findings of 44 studies conducted between 1918 and 1970. The researchers used a single criterion of success: remaining in the community as opposed to returning to an institution. Recognizing the limitations of such a cursory analysis, McCarver

FIGURE II.1
RESIDENT POPULATION OF PUBLIC INSTITUTIONS
FY 71-72 Through FY 75-76

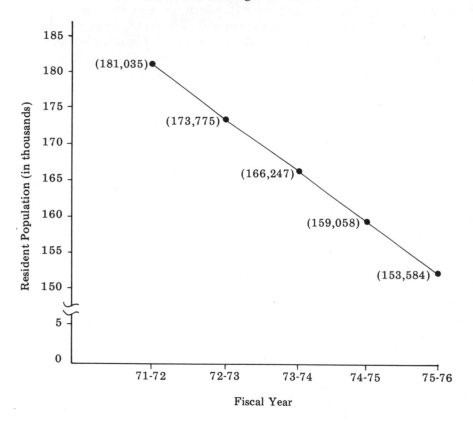

Source: R.C. Scheerenberger, *Public Residential Services for the Mentally Retarded,* 1976, National Association of Superintendents of Public Residential Facilities for the Mentally Retarded.

and Craig used it solely as a means for summarizing the rate of "success" in a diverse group of studies. They calculated a success rate of
about 69 percent, based on 9,116 subjects in the 44 studies. When
they divided the studies into four time periods, the success rates were
72 percent from 1918 to 1935; 89 percent from 1936 to 1953; 65
percent from 1954 to 1959; and 53 percent from 1960 to 1970.

McCarver and Craig offer an explanation for the declining success
rates since 1953 which is particularly relevant to the results reported
in this book. They point to the increasing complexity of society and

the decreasing capabilities of the people released into communities as possible explanations for the lower success rates; that is, while communities have become more difficult to live in, people who are released from institutions have a reduced capacity for adjusting. While this seems a reasonable explanation, it begs the issue of what is meant by decreased ability and the extent to which the situation is amenable to remedies.

Despite the apparently lower success rates in more recent years, the conclusion still holds that most individuals do reasonably well in the community. This has been a relatively consistent finding, although there appears to be some hesitation both among the public at large and within many professional circles to believe that mentally retarded people are in fact capable of "making it" in the community.

This tendency toward disbelief was sharply illustrated in the public reaction to the first significant study of the community adjustment of mentally retarded persons. Walter Fernald in 1919 studied inmates who had escaped or were reluctantly discharged from Waverly State School in Massachusetts during the period from 1890 to 1914. Fernald himself expected to discover that the retarded people were not only adjusting poorly but were engaging in harmful or destructive behavior in the community. His attitude toward retarded people at the time he conducted the study is reflected in an excerpt from a paper he presented at the National Conference of Charities and Correction in 1904:

> No method of training or discipline can fit them to become safe or desirable members of society. They cannot be "placed out" without great moral risk to innocent people. These cases should be recognized at an early age before they have acquired facility in actual crime and permanently taken out of the community . . . .[15]

In particular, he described the dangers posed by mentally retarded women:

> Feebleminded women are almost invariably immoral and if at large, usually become carriers of venereal disease or give birth to children who are as defective as themselves . . . .[16]

Despite his expectations to the contrary, Fernald found that the retarded people he studied were doing well in the community and had not committed a disproportionate number of crimes; indeed, most had merged into the general population. According to Davies, it was "little short of a revelation" that "there was found among the women subjects, no preponderant amount of delinquency, so few illegitimate children, and so few children in general, that many were good wives, and that many more were materially contributing to their maintenance."[17]

Studies comparing the community adjustment experiences of retarded and nonretarded people have yielded several interesting findings. These studies have shown that the community experiences of retarded people are very similar to those of nonretarded individuals. For example, Ruby Kennedy noted that the overwhelming majority of both retarded and nonretarded individuals he studied had made acceptable and remarkably similar adjustment in the personal, social, and economic spheres.[18] Where the retarded people tended to score lower on certain dimensions, these differences were generally considered to reflect the degree rather than the kind of adjustment. For example, Kennedy found that the retarded people studied were slightly less active in their participation in social activities, but the types of activities in which they participated were similar to those in which nonretarded individuals took part.

It is important to note, however, that all is not rosy. Although most researchers found that a majority of the people seemed to be doing well, a significant number were *not* successful in their adjustment to the community. Also, of those who adjusted well according to the various criteria used in the studies, several levels of adjustment are apparent *within* the sample groups.

Social adjustment frequently entails the greatest problems for mentally retarded persons, as illustrated in Gerhart Saenger's follow-up study of 520 mentally retarded adults who were former pupils in New York City classes for the "trainable retarded."[19] He found that only half of the group were reported to have friends, one-quarter had friends of the opposite sex, and one-third were able to leave their immediate neighborhood or take buses and subways by themselves. Similarly, Camille Lambert summarized the findings of his follow-up study of 373 persons living in Ontario:

> About one-half of these adults had never worked . . . . Most of them do very little around the house, and scarcely participate in activities in the home or outside of it . . . . Some of the barriers which they identified to a more full participation in life were the absence of other persons to help them around in the community and the scarcity of other people with whom they might interact . . . .[20]

Obviously, the community adjustment of mentally retarded persons has not been a complete success story. As Edgar Doll, developer of the Vineland Social Maturity Scale and one of the forefathers in the field of mental retardation, observed in 1932:

> What becomes of the non-institutionalized feebleminded? Many of them continue to receive financial support and social supervision of their families so successfully that they do not become social problems outside of their homes. On the other hand, neither do they become social successes. They live in a sort of purgatory between success and

failure, rising and falling with the tide of circumstances . . . apparently, they find some humble niche in society which they can fill without becoming such a social menace that society becomes gravely concerned about them.[21]

Robert Edgerton also emphasizes the social isolation which many mentally retarded persons experience when living in the community — particularly the stigma of being regarded as mentally inferior and the intense need to pass as "normal." He concluded in his study: "These former patients have not become pillars of society, but neither have they been conspicuous in their opposition to social norms or to law." [22]

In his follow-up study about 12 years later Edgerton found that "concern with stigma was far less evident . . . What seemed to dominate their interests was not work or stigma . . . but recreation, hobbies, leisure, good times, friends and family . . . The majority of them felt happier now than before."[23] In general the people Edgerton writes about changed considerably during the 12 years between the two studies, but were generally better blended into the community as the distance between them and their institutional experiences increased.

The findings of all these studies substantiate Doll's belief that the community experiences of mentally retarded people constitute a "purgatory between success and failure." Many mentally retarded persons manage to exist and "make it" in the community but the quality of their lives has been deficient in many respects, and the problems of adjustment persist.

Fernald was so surprised by the results of his study and aware of their controversial implications that he hesitated for two years before publishing his findings. The results of other studies, similar in nature to Fernald's conclusions, have seemed less shocking as society's attitudes toward mentally retarded people have changed and awareness of both their capabilities and their rights has grown. Despite these changes, however, some are still skeptical of positive reports of community adjustment and others are equally skeptical when difficulties are reported. We hope that the findings presented in this book shed additional light not only on the question of whether retarded people can make it in the community, but also on the complex problems of adjustment and specific factors which seem to contribute to more or less successful experiences in *coming back*.

DEINSTITUTIONALIZATION: SOME PERSPECTIVES

Unfortunately, a simple reduction in the census of an institution does not automatically imply that a mentally retarded person is no longer in an institutional setting. Frequently it simply means a transfer to another institutional setting, such as a mental hospital or a nursing home. For the purposes of this book, the term "deinstitutionalization" refers to the release of a mentally retarded person from an institution to a community setting. A community is defined as including family settings (natural, adoptive, or foster homes); group homes; cooperative apartments and other semi-independent living situations; and various independent living arrangements for mentally retarded persons, such as apartments or boarding homes. We realize that many community-based residences are considered by some observers to be "mini-institutions" because of their restrictive and segregating characteristics. In this study, however, we are concerned with the distinction between the large-scale (over 100 residents), highly structured, often isolated, total-care facility and the smaller, less structured facility located within the community.

As the pressure to reduce the population in institutions has grown, so too has the pressure to establish community placements. Unfortunately, the pressure for release has frequently grown more rapidly than the pressure to establish residential alternatives, with the result that many mentally retarded people have been moved from one inadequate setting to another. Simultaneously, there has been a spurt of class action suits for the right of individuals in institutions to receive adequate treatment. This has placed additional pressure on institutions to meet certain minimum standards, a force often at odds with the pressure to prepare residents to enter the community. Scarce public funds are often allocated for improvements in the institutions — leaving little for the communities to use in creating alternative residences. It is within this context of conflicting pressures and strong sentiments that most instances of deinstitutionalization of mentally retarded people have taken place.

A number of studies are being conducted to determine what factors within the institution, the individual, and the community affect the adjustment of the mentally retarded person. In the current study we refrain from judging the community experiences of mentally retarded people in terms of success and failure, nor do we assume that those individuals experiencing difficulty adjusting should be back in the institutions.

Deinstitutionalization should be viewed as both a social phenomenon and a social policy.[24] As an event in the life of a mentally retarded person the process entails a migration from the closed society of the institution to the open and more complex society of the community.

The process of deinstitutionalization will be successful only if preceded by three kinds of preparation: institutions must be prepared to release mentally retarded persons, these individuals must be prepared for their release, and communities must be prepared to receive them. Frequently, these preparatory steps succumb to a variety of political, economic, organizational, and social constraints. Institutions are often not prepared to release mentally retarded people, the people are not considered ready for release, and communities are unprepared to receive them. Yet, deinstitutionalization is occurring. Institutions in many cases resist it; indeed, because of funding streams, they are given incentives to resist.[25] Some claim that inadequately prepared individuals have been "dumped" into communities which lack the support services to receive new residents. Each of these prerequisites for the successful release of individuals to community settings is explored in more detail below.

Institutional Preparation

The ability of the institution to prepare for and adjust to its changing role has been referred to in the Developmentally Disabled Assistance and Bill of Rights Act (PL 94-103) as "institutional reform." An example is a staff retraining program designed to prepare employees to assume new roles either within or outside the institution. The institution might also take part in preparing its residents for eventual release into the community. Indeed, decisions regarding release and community placement have traditionally been made by personnel within the institution. Institutional staff frequently judge the individual's readiness for the move, as well as the community's ability to receive the individual. The effective transition from one agency (the institution) to another (the community agency or residence) in many cases entails both a physical move and a transfer of the responsibility for ensuring continued service. Many individuals placed in the community are not formally discharged from the institution; thus, the institution continues to have some legal responsibility for the individual's care. If a released individual has difficulty adjusting to the community setting, the institution tends to be considered a back-up residential option, used with greater or lesser frequency in different states. In other words, the institution and the community can be considered closely linked components of the same service delivery system.

There are, however, many problems inherent in the process of changing institutional roles. State institutions for mentally retarded persons have existed for many more years than community-based programs. Public mandates are relatively consistent from state to state but have shifted over the past hundred years, as we have described. Institutions were originally established to train mentally retarded persons and return them to the community. Later, the purpose was to remove from the community those mentally retarded individuals considered to be potentially dangerous. This objective was subsequently modified when institutions were thought to be appropriate for *most* mentally retarded persons, especially the severely retarded population. In recent years the full circle has been completed, and institutions are again being seen as part of a continuum of services, with a potentially important role in training persons for life in the community. (Interestingly, current reasons for institutionalizing an individual sometimes emphasize the person's abilities and needs and sometimes those of the community.) If an individual is considered unable to function in the community, and if the community has no appropriate or adequate services for that individual, the decision may still be made to place the person in an institution.

The pressure on institutions to shift roles — to become active and transitional participants in rehabilitating mentally retarded persons rather than providing them with permanent custodial care — has caused some tension because of the traditional mandates of these institutions. Financial support of persons in institutions is often provided in a pattern which promotes the institution's custodial and habilitation mandates. While resources for custodial care usually are allocated evenly among the population of an institution, habilitation resources are sometimes selectively distributed so that maximum success is gained with individuals who are considered "good risks." Such policies, which establish that services are to be provided to those most likely to be successfully rehabilitated, result from pressures on administrators and program managers to demonstrate that the mandates for active habilitation and treatment are being addressed. National and state organizations, such as the Association for Retarded Citizens, demand that the institutions serve the individual needs of each person. On the other hand, both the general public and the state legislatures demand the economy and are often reluctant to provide the resources necessary to meet long-term needs. The very nature of the institution requires that it both habilitate and maintain clients, but such habilitation and maintenance efforts may conflict with program development.

Individual Preparation

Considerable emphasis has traditionally been placed on preparing the individual for the move to the community. It is increasingly recognized, however, that with an adequate support structure in the community, few, if any, mentally retarded persons need ever be sent to an institution, and most, if not all, currently institutionalized persons can be released. Returning to the community, as opposed to never leaving it, presents additional complications: a person who has lived in an institution for many years not only has much learning to do, but also a considerable emount of unlearning. Thus, the deinstitutionalization process can be difficult, especially for many older mentally retarded persons.

Community Preparation

An emerging notion underlying current efforts to move people out of the institution and into the community is that an essential part of community adjustment is the community's ability to provide support for the mentally retarded person. Given an adequate community support structure, most mentally retarded individuals could readily adjust to life in the community, and most families could be a major source of continued community support. An adequate community support structure must provide at least three kinds of support. First, a variety of *residential options* must be available for mentally retarded persons, in addition to living with the natural family, living independently, or living in the institution. Increasingly, this means adding options beyond the traditional "community residence" of group homes, "cooperative apartments," and "foster care." ENCOR (Eastern Nebraska Community Office of Retardation), for example, tailors the residential setting to the needs of the individual rather than trying to fit the individual into a predesigned setting.

Second, *supportive services* must be provided. These may include day care, training, education, sheltered employment, recreation, counseling, protective and other social services, information and referral services, follow-up services, transportation, and education.

Third, *preventive and early intervention services* must be available to reduce the likelihood that a person will need to be removed from a family setting. These services should encompass early diagnosis, evaluation, prescription, and treatment.

Beyond offering a full array of residential options and services, community support must be provided within the context of a comprehensive system of service delivery. In order to meet all the needs of the mentally retarded individual who has been released to the community, services offered by various agencies must be coordinated.

The degree to which institutions and individuals are prepared for the process of transition to the community varies tremendously across the country; and the growth of community support systems is uneven. Nevertheless, people are being released from institutions, and studies of their experiences are being conducted, in an effort to develop a better understanding of the challenges of the future. The following chapters, which describe the experiences of mentally retarded people living in the midst of these changes, hopefully convey the complexity of growth and adaptation to a new life by those most directly involved.

REFERENCES

1. Stanley P. Davies, *The Mentally Retarded in Society* (New York: Columbia University Press, 1959), p. 23.

2. Wolf Wolfensberger, *The Origin and Nature of our Institutional Models* (Syracuse: Syracuse University Center on Human Policy, 1974), p. 31.

3. David J. Rothman, *The Discovery of the Asylum: Social Order and Disorder in the New Republic* (Boston: Little Brown and Co., 1971), p. 180.

4. Davies, pp. 23-24.

5. Wolf Wolfensberger, *The Origin and Nature of our Institutional Models.*

6. Davies, p. 42.

7. Wolf Wolfensberger, *The Origin and Nature of our Institutional Models,* p. 47.

8. Davies, pp. 115-119.

9. Wolf Wolfensberger, *The Principle of Normalization in Human Services* (Toronto: National Institute on Mental Retardation, 1972), p. 28.

10. Ibid., p. 92

11. E. Butterfield, "Some Basic Changes in Residential Facilities," in Robert B. Kugel and Ann Shearer, eds., *Changing Patterns in Residential Services for the Mentally Retarded* (Washington, D.C.: President's Committee on Mental Retardation, 1976), pp. 15-16.

12. Report to Congress by the Comptroller General of the United States, *Returning the Mentally Disabled to the Community: Government Needs to Do More* (Washington, D.C.: January 1977), p. 9.

13. Bengt Nirge, "The Normalization Principle and its Human Management Implications," in Robert B. Kugel and Wolf Wofensberger, ed., *Changing Patterns in Residential Services for the Mentally Retarded,* President's Committee on Mental Retardation, Washington, D.C., 1969, p. 181.

14. R. McCarver and E. Craig, "Placement of the Retarded in the Community: Prognosis and Outcome," *International Review of Research in Mental Retardation,* 7 (1974): 145-207.

15. Walter Fernald, "Care of the Feeble-minded," (Boston: George H. Ellis Co., 1912), p. 7; reprinted from *National Bulletin of Charities and Corrections* (1904), pp. 380-390.

16. Ibid., p. 5.

17. Davies, p. 110.

18. Ruby Kennedy, *A Connecticut Community Revisited: A Study of the Social Adjustment of a Group of Mentally Deficient Adults in 1948 and 1960*, a report on Project No. 655 to the Office of Vocational Rehabilitation (Washington, D.C.: Department of Health, Education and Welfare, 1962).

19. Gerhart Saenger, *The Adjustment of Severely Retarded Adults in the Community*, a report to the New York State Interdepartmental Health Resources Board (Albany: October 1957).

20. Camille Lambert, "Profiles of Adults Living in the Community," paper presented at the Oxford Symposium on the Adult Retarded in Ontario: Today and Tomorrow, September 1974, Woodstock, Ontario, p. 15.

21. Kennedy, p. 70.

22. Robert B. Edgerton, *The Cloak of Competence: Stigma in the Lives of the Mentally Retarded* (Berkeley, California: University of California Press, 1967), p. 142.

23. Robert B. Edgerton and Sylvia M. Bercouici,"The Cloak of Competence: Years Later," *American Journal of Mental Deficiency* (1976), Volume 80, No. 5, pp. 485-497.

24. According to the U.S. Department of Health, Education and Welfare, an average of approximately 15,000 mentally retarded persons are released annually from institutions in the nation. Note that this figure refers to the total numbers of individuals released, not only those released to community settings, as defined in this study.

25. William Goldman, "Community Services: The Only Salvation of Deinstitutionalization," presented at Management Training Program, University of Alabama, 1974 (mimeographed).

Chapter III
Who Are They?

Our purpose in writing this book is to describe the experiences of people who, after years of living in an institution, were released to live in the community. It is tempting to think of these people as newcomers to the community but they are not newcomers at all; at one time they were members of the community, then for various reasons they were placed in institutions. In retrospect, their removal from the community may have been unnecessary, and in recognition of this, measures are being taken to make it possible for them to come back, to return to the community.

This chapter describes some of the characteristics of the study group members: their age, sex, appearance, level of retardation, and additional disabilities. Their institutional experiences are also described, including their institutional history and the training they received. The material presented in this chapter, as well as the chapters which follow, is organized around two major dimensions: age and level of retardation. The descriptions of the people and their institutional experiences will provide a backdrop against which their community experiences can be understood and evaluated.

As noted earlier (see Chapter I), we conducted a survey of public and private institutions serving mentally retarded people throughout the country. A total of 154 institutions responded (out of 250 which were contacted). These institutions had released a total of over 13,000 individuals to community placements. All these individuals met the same criteria as those finally selected for the study reported here: they were between the ages of 6 and 40 at the time of their release, had been institutionalized for at least two years prior to release, and were released to community settings (not to other institutional settings). The survey results indicate that the study group we describe here is representative of the larger population of individuals released to the community.[1]

INDIVIDUAL CHARACTERISTICS

Age, Sex, and Level of Retardation

The people included in this study were all between the ages of five and 51 years at the time of the interviews; 19 percent (84) were 18 years or younger (referred to here as children), while 81 percent (356) were 19 years or older (adults). Only 7 percent of the people were more than 40 years of age.* Forty-one percent of the children and 46 percent of the adults were female.

Those who returned to the community represented all levels of retardation although persons with lesser disabilities were in the great majority. Measures of level of retardation were based on I.Q. scores grouped into four categories: mild (I.Q. = 68-52), moderate (I.Q. = 51-36), severe (I.Q. = 35-20), and profound (I.Q. = 19 or less).[2] Only 5 percent of the group were moderately retarded, whereas 41 percent were mildly retarded. Because so few were profoundly retarded the categories of severe and profound levels of retardation were merged and will be referred to as "severe" throughout the book.

The proportion of males increased with the level of retardation. As Table III.1 shows, about 51 percent of the mildly retarded were males, while 56 percent of the moderately retarded and 57 percent of

TABLE III.1
SEX AND LEVEL OF RETARDATION

Level of Retardation

| Sex | Mild | | Moderate | | Severe | | Total [a] | |
	N(171)	%	N(137)	%	N(106)	%	N(414)	%
Male	87	51	76	56	60	57	223	54
Female	84	49	61	44	46	43	191	46

[a] Throughout the tables presented in this book, small variations exist in the numbers reported as "N" and as "totals." These variations were caused by differing response rates to each item. Unless otherwise noted, percentages refer to the group for which information was available — not to the total study group. "N" refers to the number of study group members about whom information was obtained.

* As noted above, the original study plan was to include persons between the ages of six and 40, but the actual ages of participants ranged from five to 51. The small number of persons older than 40 is likely a result of the original study plan.

the severely retarded were males. Children and adults were also differentially distributed in relation to level of retardation: 42 percent of the children, compared with only 22 percent of the adults, were in the severe category. (See Table III.2.)

TABLE III.2
AGE AND LEVEL OF RETARDATION

Level of Retardation

Age	Mild N(169)	%	Moderate N(134)	%	Severe N(106)	%	Total N(409)	%
Children	23	14	20	15	31	29	74	18
Adults	146	86	114	85	75	71	335	82

Appearance

Appearance is an important component of acceptance as a "normal" participant in community life. Persons who have spent a considerable period of time in institutional settings may be more likely than others to appear unusual because of general physical appearance, improper dietary regulations, and inadequate grooming or inappropriate dress. We rated the study group members on these dimensions.

About 63 percent of the group were rated as normal in terms of physical features and appearance, 33 percent were somewhat abnormal, and only 4 percent were judged to be *very* abnormal. Weight was not generally a problem. Only 8 percent were judged to be very overweight and only 4 percent unusually underweight, whereas 88 percent were within normal weight ranges. In terms of grooming and dress, most were rated as well groomed and properly dressed by the interviewers. Table III.3 shows that more than 80 percent of the people were rated as good in every category except general appearance and 79 percent were classified as good in that category. Very few persons were judged as poor in any category.

The fact that the great majority of the people studied were normal in virtually all aspects of their appearance may be related to two points. First, spokespersons for releasing institutions indicated that they felt it was easier to place individuals in the community who had a relatively normal appearance and this factor was likely to have influenced who was released. Second, those who were released may have

begun to dress and comport themselves more normally or more according to community expectations as a result of living in the community.
Whatever the reason, the study group as a whole was relatively normal
in appearance — an important part of fitting into a new home and community.

TABLE III.3
APPEARANCE: GROOMING AND DRESS

Grooming and Dress	Good		Fair		Poor		Total	
	N	%	N	%	N	%	N	%
Cleanliness	340	84	55	14	10	2	405	100
Fit of clothing	312	81	69	18	4	1	387	100
Clothing appropriate to age	350	90	37	9	2	1	389	100
Clothing appropriate to season	371	95	17	4	2	1	390	100
General appearance	312	79	69	18	9	3	393	100

Additional Disabilities

Individuals who are retarded frequently have additional disabilities
to cope with, and these must be taken into consideration when examining their community experiences. Most of the people who returned
to the community had additional disabilities. No information was
obtained on the severity of these handicaps, with the exception of
mobility impairments. However, even a relatively minor additional
disability is likely to compound the problems of learning to live in the
community. This is illustrated by certain remarks by interviewers
about study group members.

> Apparently L's mental retardation is not his major handicap as he is
> only a borderline MR (he can read at 6th grade level). His major handi-
> cap involves behavior problems. L's physical and verbal aggressive-
> ness while he was in the community eventually led to his return to the
> institution.

M seems very well adjusted. She is extremely articulate and thoughtful in answering questions. Her counselor said that the only thing that is handicapping her is a slight facial deformity . . . . He said she has suffered from that rather than her retardation. One would-be employer turned her down for a job because of her nose.

K was not interviewable. He is blind and nonverbal. He was playing a pipe organ while I was there — he appears to love the sound and the exercise is good for his crippled hands.

Of the 440 study group members, 59 percent had at least one additional disability and 12 percent had two or more additional disabilities.

It is interesting, though perhaps not surprising, that the presence of additional disabilities and deformities was strongly related to age and level of retardation: younger and more retarded individuals were considerably more likely to be multiply handicapped and to have deformities than older, less retarded people. (Note that the younger study group members were also more retarded.) Over 70 percent of the severely retarded people (see Table III.4) and of the children (see Table III.5) had additional disabilities, compared with somewhat over half the remainder of the population. Similarly, about one-quarter of the children and the severely retarded individuals had visible deformities compared with only about 13 percent of the rest of the study group.* Tables III.4 and III.5 show the distribution of the presence or absence of additional disabilities in the study group. (See Appendix B, Tables B.1 and B.2 for a more detailed description of the number of additional disabilities.)

We obtained information on the following categories of disabling conditions: blindness, deafness, limitations of physical mobility, speech impairments, epilepsy, psychological problems, and physical deformi-

TABLE III.4
NUMBER OF ADDITIONAL DISABILITIES BY
LEVEL OF RETARDATION

| Number of Disabilities | Level of Retardation | | | | | | | |
| | Mild | | Moderate | | Severe | | Total | |
	N(171)	%	N(137)	%	N(106)	%	N(414)	%
None	78	46	65	47	31	29	174	42
One or more	93	54	72	53	75	71	240	58

* Deformities were noted by interviewers and included deformities of the face, head, hands, arms, feet, and legs.

TABLE III.5
NUMBER OF ADDITIONAL DISABILITIES BY AGE

Number of Disabilities	Children		Adults		Total	
	N(83)	%	N(357)	%	N(440)	%
None	22	27	158	44	180	41
One or more	61	73	199	56	260	59

ties. Some disabling conditions were more common than others. Thirty-three percent of the people had speech impairments of one sort or another, 15 percent had mobility problems (only six individuals used wheelchairs and only two were confined to bed), 13 percent had psychological problems, 12 percent were epileptic, slightly less than 9 percent were either blind or deaf, and only 15 percent had visible deformities.

Tables III.6 and III.7 show the distribution of these categories of abilities among children and adults and among the three levels of retardation, respectively. Children were almost five times as likely to be blind as adults, more than twice as likely to be deaf, and a third more likely to have mobility difficulties or epilepsy. Similarly, about one-quarter of the children had visible deformities, while this was true for only 13 percent of the adults. The greater likelihood of additional disabilities and deformities among children must be taken into consideration in planning their return to the community.

In every category except psychological problems, severely retarded persons are more likely to be disabled, and in the case of deafness, mobility, and speech impairments, the likelihood of disability varies directly with the level of retardation. More than half of the severely retarded had speech impairments while one-fifth had mobility limitations.

On the surface, it might appear that a speech impairment — the most common additional disability at all levels of retardation — is a relatively minor limitation. However, it can present major difficulties in terms of social adjustment in the community and in employment and other social situations. It is interesting to note that speech therapy and training were two kinds of unmet service needs mentioned relatively frequently by families of study group members.

Another common type of additional disability was psychological problems. Unlike the other disabilities, psychological problems were reported more frequently among the older, less retarded individuals.

TABLE III.6
TYPE OF ADDITIONAL DISABILITIES BY AGE[a]

Type of Disability	Children		Adults		Total	
	N(84)	%	N(356)	%	N(440)	%
Blindness	21	25	19	5	40	9
Deafness	14	16	25	7	39	9
Mobility limitations	21	25	46	13	67	15
Speech impairment	40	47	109	31	149	34
Epilepsy	16	19	37	10	53	12
Psychological problems	12	14	45	13	57	13

TABLE III.7
TYPE OF ADDITIONAL DISABILITY BY LEVEL
OF RETARDATION[a]

	Level of Retardation							
Type of Disability	Mild		Moderate		Severe		Total	
	N(171)	%	N(137)	%	N(106)	%	N(414)	%
Blind- ness	12	7	7	5	11	10	30	7
Deafness	11	6	9	7	13	12	33	8
Mobility limita- tion	16	9	14	10	22	21	52	13
Speech im- pairment	31	18	44	32	57	54	132	32
Epilepsy	21	12	15	11	14	13	50	12
Psychological problems	28	16	16	12	10	7	54	13

---

[a] Percentages do not add up to 100 because some people had more than one additional disability. Percentages refer to the proportion of the total group with each disability.

INSTITUTIONAL EXPERIENCES

In addition to whatever personal characteristics the individuals had as they came back to the community, they also had a variety of institutional experiences which could be expected to have an impact on their return. In this section we describe some of the more important aspects of the releasing institutions, as well as the institutional histories of the study group members, and the training which they received prior to release.

Some Background on Releasing Institutions

More than two-thirds of the people (68 percent) were released from institutions which had policies that included continued responsibility for the well-being of individuals released to live in the community. Slightly less than half the individuals were released from institutions which provided training for the families of released residents, but almost 60 percent were released from institutions providing some support to day program staff (teachers and/or employers in the community). In general, then, more than half of the study group members were released from institutions which took some responsibility for preparing either the family or the community to which people were released and provided a means for maintaining involvement with the individual after release.

General Institutional Background

Virtually all members of the study group lived with their own families prior to the first commitment to an institution; only 2 percent had never lived with their families. Most of the people (44 percent) began their institutional careers as the result of a court order or through authorization by a parent or legal guardian (39 percent). A small number (11 percent) admitted themselves, while the remaining 6 percent came to the institution by a variety of other means.

Once admitted, they stayed for a considerable period of time; the average length of stay in the institution from which they were released was 10.6 years. In addition, 40 percent of the people had spent an average of 10.2 years in at least one other institution. Thus, the study group members generally had rather lengthy institutional careers prior to returning to the community.

Participation in Institutional Programs

Residents of an institution may receive a variety of services and training. Much of the training and many of the services are provided through structured programs. We obtained information about two basic types of programs: (1) structured prelease training specifically designed to prepare individuals for life in the community, and (2) day programs offered to residents in the six months prior to their release, regardless of whether they were being specifically prepared for release into the community.

Prerelease Programs. Information was obtained on four types of prerelease programs: special residential, sheltered workshop, competitive employment, and special school programs.

Special residential programs were usually semi-independent living arrangements on the grounds of the institution. The programs were individualized and emphasized experience in working in a community atmosphere and learning social and personal skills.

Sheltered workshop programs offered training in social and behavioral skills and were located on the grounds of the institution.

Competitive employment programs were designed to allow people to gain experiences in working in a competitive environment. These programs emphasized vocational skills and included community-related living skills.

Special school programs were provided for children. Some were located at the institution while others were in the community.

Table III.8 shows that the most common prerelease program in which the people who returned to the community participated was a special residential program (in which 28 percent of the total group participated); the least common was a special school program (accounting for only 3 percent of the total group). Fifty-three percent of the people did not participate in any formal prerelease program and 19 percent participated in more than one program.*

TABLE III.8
PARTICIPATION IN PRERELEASE PROGRAMS

Type of Program	Number of Participants	
	N(274)	%
Special residential	124	28
Sheltered workshop	108	25
Competitive employment	30	7
Special school	12	3

* It should be noted that one institution releasing over 100 study group members did not call any of its programs "prerelease." Therefore, about 25 percent of the study group could not have participated in such programs.

Day Programs. Four types of day programs were available to the people while institutionalized: competitive employment, sheltered employment, day activity centers, and school. Some were located on the grounds of the institution and others in the community, making a total of eight possible day program placements. In fact, none of the institutions reported offering competitive employment programs.

About three-quarters of the total group participated in some program of day placement during the six months prior to their release. A total of 22 percent participated in more than one day program. Almost 80 percent of the day placements were located on the grounds of the institution, and the remaining 20 percent were in the community. (See Appendix B, Tables B.3 and B.4). The most common day programs were sheltered workshops and schools on the grounds of the institutions (accounting for participation by 39 and 27 percent of the study group, respectively). Two-thirds of the mildly retarded individuals took part in sheltered workshops prior to release, compared to less than one-third of the severely retarded individuals. Over 60 percent of the adults but only about 5 percent of the children participated. However, over half the children took part in school programs prior to release.

TABLE III.9
NUMBER OF DAY PLACEMENTS BY AGE

Number of Programs	Children N(84)	%	Adults N(356)	%	Total N(40)	%
None	40	48	85	24	125	28
One	40	48	188	52	228	52
Two or more	4	4	83	24	87	20

TABLE III.10
NUMBER OF DAY PLACEMENTS BY LEVEL OF RETARDATION

Number of Programs	Level of Retardation							
	Mild N(165)	%	Moderate N(137)	%	Severe N(106)	%	Total N(408)	%
None	26	15	38	28	51	48	115	28
One	95	56	81	59	42	40	218	53
Two or more	44	29	18	13	13	12	75	19

Children and the severely retarded were less likely to have participated in day placements (40 and 48 percent, respectively). Tables III.9 and III.10 show participation by age and level of retardation. Only about two-thirds of the people were satisfied with prelease training, irrespective of age or level of retardation. In the case of the severely retarded, however, more than 40 percent were satisfied (see Appendix B, Tables B.5 and B.6).

Family Perceptions of Institutional Training

Whether through prerelease programs, structured day programs, or less formal training activities, training in a wide range of skills may have been provided to study group members while they were institutionalized. We identified six major categories of training.*

- personal maintenance: eating, using the toilet, dressing and undressing, cleanliness, and grooming;

- sensory development: motor, hearing and vision, and speech and language development;

- education and employment: preacademic, numbers and telling time, reading and writing, prevocational, and vocational;

- domestic living: housekeeping, meal preparation, shopping, and money management;

- use of community resources: travel and mobility, using the telephone, coping with emergencies, and using community agencies;

- behavior management: interpersonal relationships, behavior control, and social and recreational activities.

For each type of training, the family respondent was asked two questions:

- Was the training received by the mentally retarded person at the institution? If yes, was the training adequate?

- If the training was not received, was it needed? If it was not needed, was this because the individual already had the skill or was not ready for that type of training?

---

* We use the same six categories in Chapter VIII to describe training received in the community.

Personal Maintenance.   About half the study group members received various types of training in personal maintenance while institutionalized. Most of the families felt that the training was adequate,
except in regard to cleanliness. According to responses by the families,
less than 5 percent of the people needed but did not receive training
in personal maintenance. About half the study group needed no training in personal care, eating, using the toilet, or dressing because they
already had these skills, but only about one-quarter had sufficient
grooming skills, according to the family respondents. (See Appendix B,
Table B.7.)

Sensory Development.   As with personal maintenance, about half
the study group received some type of sensory development training
while institutionalized. In general, training in these areas was considered to be either less adequate or less available for those needing it
than training in personal maintenance. Speech therapy was most
frequently cited as needed but not provided, or inadequate when
provided. This finding is consistent with the fact that many study group
members had speech impairments — apparently they received inadequate attention in the institution. As we shall see in Chapter VIII,
speech training was inadequate or lacking in the community as well.

Education and Employment.   Although about half the study group
received some type of education and employment training prior to
release, about one-third of the families felt that the training was inadequate. About one-third of the study group did not need preacademic training because they already had the skills, and another third
were not considered ready for vocational training.

Domestic Living.   Over half the families felt that training in housekeeping skills was adequate. However, a similar proportion of respondents indicated that meal preparation, money management, and shopping were the skills most needed, and about half felt that the training
in these skills was not provided or if provided was inadequate.

Use of Community Resources.   Most aspects of training in use of
community resources were either needed but not provided or were
inadequate when provided. Less than 20 percent of the family respondents felt that training in this area was adequate. About half the
families responded that the study group member was not yet ready for
training in the use of community agencies. Relatively few respondents
felt that the individual was sufficiently skilled in using community
resources to eliminate the need for training.

Behavior Management.   About three-quarters of the study group
received some training in interpersonal relationships and behavior
management while institutionalized, but only about half the families
of these individuals felt that the training was adequate. The one type of

behavioral training which families most often felt was adequate was in the area of social and recreational activities. Virtually all study group members received some training of this kind and about two-thirds of the families felt that the required skills in this area were adequate.

In general, training was perceived by families as adequate in basic skill areas and inadequate in more advanced areas, including crucial skills in using community resources. When training was provided by the institution, families generally felt it was adequate, with the striking exception of behavior management training. Social and recreational training was most likely to be perceived as adequate. The study group members were thought to be most prepared in the basic aspects of personal maintenance, and least prepared in the more complicated areas of domestic, educational, vocational, and community use skills.

When asked to give their overall assessment of the prerelease preparation, about two-thirds of the family respondents indicated that they were satisfied and one-third that they were dissatisfied. Families of children and adults were about equally satisfied, but families of severely retarded individuals were considerably less satisfied than families of those who were less retarded.

Study Group Members' Perceptions of Institutional Training

We also questioned the study group members about their institutional training experiences. They were asked to indicate the kinds of training they received from the institution which helped them deal with life in the community. They responded in four areas: taking care of themselves and their home; participating in school or work; getting along with other people; and doing things in the community.

In each area they were asked two questions:

What did you learn that was helpful?

What do you wish you had learned?

Figure III.1 through III.4 list selected verbatim responses to each of these questions; they provide cogent statements by the study group members of their own perceived needs and desires.

Members of the study group felt that while they were institutionalized, self-care skills were emphasized; they were less satisfied with domestic skills relating to maintaining an apartment or preparing food. Most marked was the desire for additional training in advanced skills, including reading, writing, arithmetic, and manual activities (making repairs, typing, and the like). They also felt more training should have been provided in dealing with money and in the skills necessary to purchase such basic items as food and clothing. Perhaps most perceptive was their awareness of the need for greater skills in getting along with other people in the community. Thus, responses by the study group members parallel those of their families: training in the basic skills related to personal care was adequate, whereas the more advanced intellectual and manual skills and those required to participate in the community and interact with other people were under-emphasized.

FIGURE III.1
INSTITUTIONAL SELF-CARE TRAINING

What did the institution teach you which helps you take care of your-self and your home?

We had to do chores — make beds, sweep floor, get up in time — get our pills and brush our teeth.

We learned to go shopping. We learned to brush our teeth three times a day. We learned to dust and clean our rooms. We learned to get up on the first call.

At the institution they taught me how to put on clothes, get zipper up and down. They taught me how to wash my hair. They taught me to trim my nails.

They taught me how to take care of myself, to do my hair. I learned to take care of my room. I learned how to spend my money.

To be yourself; cooking.

I was taking care of kids — giving them baths and I was taking a bath every day. I worked on the "X" building for four years. I worked on "Z" building — be just like this place, you have to clean the floor only you use mops to clean them out. I shaved twice a day for six months every two days and I take baths, seven times a week, seven days out of a week. Then I use deodorant seven days a week and I use shaving lotion seven days a week.

Did go to occupational therapy — sewing, making rugs, and stuff like that. No go to homemaking. They didn't teach us anything like they should. Didn't learn us anything.

It taught me to put on clean clothes every day and they taught me how to read and a little adding and subtracting, but not much 'cause I don't know how to count money back from people in the stores. I just take that as mine.

I don't think they ever taught me anything. I didn't know how to cook or anything like that when I got out of the institution. Mary, case-worker, had her secretary teach me cooking.

Is there anything you wish the institution had taught you to help you take care of yourself and your home?

I don't know. As long as I've been a patient out there I've been pretty dumb. If I would have stayed out of jail long enough they would have.

They could have told me if I ever go out and have my own apartment how to keep it clean. They could have taught me how to take care of the garbage, empty the trash. Keep my bathrooms and bedrooms clean. How to go about washing dishes, if I was living alone.

They should have a bike shop, TV shops — we could learn to fix them.

If they would help me, but they never did. I learned more here than there. Some of us kids know how to do things. A lot of things — how to set tables and schooling.

One thing — like I wasn't wishing, I was hoping they wouldn't turn those people against me when I went out there, but it didn't do no good at all.

I do enough for myself.

How to make coffee. How to make toast.

How to iron my clothes.

I do things myself. I take care of myself.

Wish they had taught me to cook better.

Wish they had better teachers, to teach cooking with meat and pota-toes, those that are capable instead of packages.

To read a bit better, I can't read much. To hunt, karate. That's mostly all. But the law, I'd like to learn if I had to go to court.

FIGURE III.2
INSTITUTIONAL SCHOOL AND WORK TRAINING

What did the institution teach you which helps you in school or at work?

Reading, spelling, and arithmetic. At first I worked with kids, then I got tired and went to food service. I dished up jello and salads.

We took tours in school and had to tell our teacher what we remembered. We learned first aid and had tests on it. We had to listen carefully to movies. We did exercises in class once a week. In the summer, we worked in the garden and learned which was weeds and which was plants.

They taught me arithmetic, color, school books. School book stuff.

I learned how to write, how to do arithmetic, reading. I learned how to make things — picture frames, churches from ice cream sticks. I learned how to make beds, and how to clean the restroom.

They taught me how to wash my hands every day — they taught me how to be on my job on time and they taught me how to dress neat when I went to work.

They didn't do nothing. It's like talking to the wall at the institution.

Nothing much — they only taught me how to do dishes.

Taking care of kids, handicapped and that. I didn't went to school, only gym.

Clean toilet, sink, empty garbage, sweep floor. If my hands were steady, I could do more.

Math and everything. They do good for me -- I appreciate it.

To do different things like tell time. Some kind of work.

How to write my name, tie my shoes.

No, they never taught me anything there.

In the workshop. Make pens, car parts, any job that came in they taught.

Send up to night school, took a cooking class. Arithmetic, reading, and graduation.

Fix bicycles, build stuff like candle holders, coat racks, make wallets, pump gas, electronics. I worked over maintenance, change diapers, and feed babies with bottles.

Is there anything you wish the institution had taught you to help you in school or at work?

I don't know what you're talking about. They taught me everything I needed to know about work, how to get there on time, how to catch the right bus to get there.

Wish they would have taught me how to multiply and divide a lot more. I have a little problem with that, but I'll get the hang of it pretty soon. They would have taught me more about working in different places. When I have problems how to sit down and talk to boss instead of blowing up.

I'd like to be a mechanic. I love cars. They could have asked me what I wanted to be if I ever got out into the community or outside of the workshop.

Train you to drive, fix cars, typing, machinery work. Don't have right teacher — should be more experienced.

If they taught me in school I would get somewhere. Working on high school diploma so I can be nurse's aide. Dad want me nurse's aide.

Read and write.

Like work, I learned on my own. Working I love — I wouldn't give it up if they'd had a school out there, I would have went. I love reading. I wouldn't give up reading. I asked the principal if I could have about five hours in school.

How to run the washer and the dryer. Using an elevator.

How to budget my money. How to spend my money wisely.

How to write. How to read.

To read better, do math better. Make TV sets and stuff, paint better.

FIGURE III.3
INSTITUTIONAL TRAINING IN INTERPERSONAL RELATIONS

What did the institution teach you to help you get along with other people?

Not to hit people, 'cause I did once, and I got on restriction.

We had a Community Living class, teaching us how to get along with people.

They taught me how to behave by getting after me. They got after me if I didn't get along.

I had classes teaching getting along with people.

How to control my temper.

I have to talk nice to the other kids.   I was always their friend out there.

Well, sometimes, they not help you with that. I always go to my case-worker. No, nope, I learned everything when I came up here.

To be nice to them and not to hang around people that's bad, because you might be bad too.

I've got to say there, too, nothing. I've got a quick temper and someone just say something to me and I just lost it.

A little. Be nice, Heck with it. I do like I want.

Yes, be friendly. Try to get along with some of them, can't get along with too many of them.

Tell ya — stay in line, do what told, go get your tray. Once I was out of line, told him get back in line.

Ya. Be friends.

Be kind. To get along with people that are blind or can't talk.

Yes. Have manners.

When I washing dishes, one of the guys said Mrs. X wants you. I said "What did I do wrong now?" She said you're going home tomorrow. I didn't believe it. I was tickled pink. Yes, they taught us how to get along with other people and not to fight. If we fought they put us in seclusion rooms. I wasn't in it, thank God, the boys in it said it was torture. *They give you a little piece of meat, potato and that's all. I used to get in trouble but I never got in that seclusion room. That's all I guess.*

Is there anything you wish the institution had taught you to help you get along with other people?

No ma'am, they was my friends out there — there wasn't anything they had to teach me. You had to be friends out there 'cause you wasn't going anyplace, except to work, and most of them worked the same place I did.

No. I get along just fine, except for one person that's a new guy that just started. I don't like him. He thinks I'm dumb, I guess.

Oh, they could have taught me to get along with people and to get acquainted a little better.

Sometimes hard. Some kids turn people in for trouble.

Yeah, I wish they did teach you how to get along with other people. They didn't.

If a person fair with me, I be same with them. I have no family, no money. If some people had to live my life, they couldn't do it, but I'm used to it.

If they would have taught me that the world would be in better shape. When I was put there, there were five blacks and 300 whites. Out of all of us black people, they wouldn't do anything for us, so we decided to get out on our own and hunt for a job — but it's getting worse once again. Most of the kids I know are out of the institution. I told John, anyone from XXX I didn't want to see. I was at a hostel one day and I went to bed at 7:30 and they claim I was stealing, so I told them to go to hell. For a while I thought they would be OK, but they got worse, so I decided to quit.

How to make friends. Sharing things.

How to be friends with people.

To act pretty good.

FIGURE III.4
INSTITUTIONAL COMMUNITY TRAINING

What did the institution teach you which helps you do things in the community?

I don't think they taught us that much — 'cause the attendants had to go with us shopping. We could never go on our own. Guess they thought we wouldn't get back. I'm never going to go back there again.

There wasn't too much they taught us. People came out and put in programs for us and left us pop. They taught us to remember our sizes when we went shopping.

How to get along with people. To realize other people have problems besides myself.

They didn't teach me anything about the community. I had to learn it on my own.

Some social workers taught me right and wrong.

I had to learn myself to do things on my own. They don't help you or nothing.

Go to church — make new friends. I go around the neighborhood. I babysit sometimes — play with kids.

The institution didn't teach me a thing. If it wasn't for John Jones, Mrs. Smith, Ed Brown, I wouldn't have learned nothing.

One day I went to hamburger stand, went to pick up phonograph. Have to change clothes to clean ones, look neat when going into town.

How to spend money.

How to shop. We worked the grounds — left the grounds and get a cab to go shopping.

Raking leaves.

You have to live on own. I didn't like my first home — I got scared. The people left me alone with 10-year-old boy — went back to institution. Was afraid someone would break in — a rich neighborhood. I don't like rich neighborhoods.

Learned to embroider designs on my clothes. Mop floors, paint, stack things high, baseball, basketball, swim, skiing, ice skate, roller skate, hockey. Count my money, buy my clothes, to use road map, hike, and fish. Back my clothes. To go the street on the bus. How to save my money.

I worked in the dining room. I went to a home ec class. I learned to look at the menus to see what would be good to make. I worked on laundry and that taught me to do washing and stuff. I mostly helped the other kids, some fell back on me, I enjoyed helping those who can't do much for themselves. My mom is in a nursing home, I used to take care of her so I had a lot of experience in taking care of people. They taught me math, reading and writing, spelling. I got a chance to go to night school. We start next month to night school. They taught me a little about money situations. They taught me grooming, keeping clean and stuff. They taught me not to get in arguments and to keep my temper down. They taught me to listen when people explain and not go against what they say. They taught me more about money so I could get the rent paid and all the bills paid. Sometimes I have trouble spelling. That's about all.

They taught me to wax floors. Wish they had taught me to fix furniture, like if a chair breaks, so I wouldn't have to depend on someone else to do it.

I went down there to go school but they didn't teach me. They came here and told me and my parents they would find me a job right away. Also said I'd go to a dance every Friday night. That wasn't true either. They put me to work finally. Know how much you got pay? $ .50 for the whole time. Paint rollers was the best thing I like. No they didn't teach me to read and write and that's the truth, too.

Is there anything you wish the institution had taught you to help you do things in the community?

Yes, I wish they would have but they didn't — only thing when our time was up they just turned us loose and we were told where to go to live — they just put us in a car and tell us we're going to a house in [community] and we have to figure it all out.

No. I think that I can go out and buy my own clothes and manage pretty well, though.

They did teach me cooking, do the dishes, take turns.

Should help me learn to subtract money [make change]. How to travel — where you're going, how much money it takes. Teach you how not to get ripped off — pickpockets steal your money.

If they just show us kids how to do things, but they don't. Glad I'm away from there.

I wish they had taught me how to use stores.

They should have taught me about the town and what it would be like to live on your own, what the outside would be like, before I went out.

Few things, like controlling my temper — getting along with other people — everyone I try working with — it isn't doing no good — they don't want my help because they think I'm crazy. You know, if I was crazy, I'd go to the hospital myself, but I'm not crazy, whatever — I don't tell people too much about myself. People around here want to know about myself, but I just can't tell them. I just can't sit around and tell them.

To help us not get lost.

How to shop for myself. Taking buses.

Nothing. I help myself.

How to work a TV.

SUMMARY

Most of the people who returned to the community were adults who were mildly or moderately retarded. About one-quarter of the study group members were severely or profoundly retarded, and about one-fifth were children. Children were more likely than adults to be severely retarded, and were also considerably more likely to have multiple handicaps and deformities. The group was about evenly divided between males and females. In general, individuals were normal in appearance.

Study group members had spent considerable periods of time in institutions prior to release, averaging 10 years at the releasing institutions, but most individuals had also lived with their families prior to being institutionalized. At the institutions, most of the study group members had received some type of training in formal prerelease or day programs, generally located on the grounds of the institution; about one-fifth of the people were trained in programs located in the communities. Training was generally perceived by both families and the retarded persons as adequate in basic self-care skills, and inadequate in more advanced areas of training, such as academic and community skills.

In terms of self-care, the study group members seemed satisfied with the training they had received while institutionalized, although several would have liked to learn more about cooking. A number of them wanted to learn more advanced academic skills, such as reading, writing, and math. They also desired more training in spending and managing money wisely, and in driving a car. Many said they wished they had learned to get along better with people.

REFERENCES

1. For a more detailed comparison of the national survey, and the study group, see Marty Wyngaarden and Elinor Gollay, "Profile of National Deinstitution-alization Patterns, 1972-1974," (Cambridge, Mass.: Abt Associates, 1976).

2. The I.Q. ranges were provided by the institutions from which the study group members were released; procedures for categorizing I.Q. ranges were those presented in the *AAMD Manual on Terminology and Classification in Mental Retardation,* Special Publication Series, No. 2, 1974.

Chapter IV
Where Are They Living?

Without a satisfactory place to live, the retarded person is unlikely to leave the institution; and once in the community, the quality of the experience is likely to depend in large part on the residence. Most of the information reported in this book was obtained from the families with whom the mentally retarded persons lived in the community. While in some instances, the respondents were actually the natural families, more often they were individuals who were paid to be responsible for the mentally retarded people, such as group home managers or foster families. In a few instances, the respondent was the mentally retarded person's social worker.

Information on the residential experience is reported in three sections. First, we describe the characteristics of the residences in which the study group members were living at the time of the study. The characteristics are in turn divided into four categories: type of setting, people living in the setting, physical attributes of the residence, and characteristics of the home's relationship to the community. Second, we describe the experiences of mentally retarded individuals in their residences, including that which they liked and disliked about their new homes. And third, we present an overall view of their residential experience since leaving the institution, including information on initial placements, number of moves, and reasons for moving.

CHARACTERISTICS OF CURRENT RESIDENCES

The residences to which people moved were categorized as follows:

- Natural/adoptive homes (referred to as natural homes);
- Foster homes;
- Group homes (settings in which no more than 25 residents were under the supervision of live-in house managers);
- Semi-independent settings (similar to group homes except that the house managers did not provide 24-hour supervision; these settings were often designed to prepare residents for independent living, e.g., cooperative apartments);
- Independent living settings (settings in which individuals lived independently; i.e., without residential staff supervision, but perhaps with social workers available as needed).

Group homes were the most common setting for the study group as a whole, as well as for each of the subgroups; but adults were somewhat more likely than children, and severely retarded more likely than less retarded persons, to be in group homes. (See Tables IV.1 and IV.2.) The second most common type of residence was the foster home; almost one-fifth of the people lived in this type of setting. Another 14 percent were living with their natural families.

TABLE IV.1
RESIDENTIAL SETTING BY AGE

Setting	Children		Adults		Total	
	N(83)	%	N(357)	%	N(440)	%
Natural parent	25	30	36	10	61	14
Foster parent	23	28	55	16	78	18
Group home	34	41	175	49	209	48
Semi-independent	1	1	44	12	45	10
Independent	—	—	47	13	47	10

There were some variations by age and level of retardation. Children were more likely than adults to live in foster homes or with their natural families. As expected, adults were more likely to live in semi-dependent or independent settings.

TABLE IV.2
RESIDENTIAL SETTING BY LEVEL OF RETARDATION

Setting	Level of Retardation							
	Mild		Moderate		Severe		Total	
	N(171)	%	N(137)	%	N(106)	%	N(414)	%
Natural parent	20	12	10	8	27	25	57	14
Foster parent	25	15	29	21	15	14	69	17
Group home	71	41	73	53	58	55	202	49
Semi-independent	21	12	14	10	6	6	41	10
Independent	34	20	11	8	—	—	45	10

The pattern of residence by level of retardation is more difficult to interpret. Moderately retarded persons were most likely to live in foster homes, were the least likely to live with their natural parents, and were almost as likely as mildly retarded people to live semi-independently. Severely retarded people were the most likely to live with their natural families, but children were even more likely than the severely retarded to live with their natural families. The high proportion of severely retarded people living in their natural homes is perhaps explained by the fact that a disproportionately large number of children were severely retarded. Apart from that association, individuals of both age groups and all levels of retardation were distributed among the different types of residence, except for independent settings. Thus, although there were some differences according to age and level of retardation, certain settings were not the exclusive domain of certain types of people. Undoubtedly, many other factors, such as the willingness and ability of natural families to accept their children and the availability of various types of residential settings, influenced the kinds of placements at least as much as age and level of retardation.

Although the kind of setting is important, other aspects of the homes in which retarded people are living are perhaps even more important. We have grouped these aspects into three categories: the characteristics of the family, the physical characteristics of the house, and the access which the house provides to the community.

Characteristics of the Family

About half of the study group members lived in settings with eight or fewer residents, 31 percent lived in homes with more than eight persons, and 18 percent lived with more than 12 other family members. Table IV.3 confirms the fact that most of the deinstitutionalized people lived in dwellings that consisted of rather large families.

TABLE IV.3
NUMBER OF PERSONS IN RESIDENCE

Number of Persons	N(440)	%
0 - 1	27	6
2 - 4	92	21
5 - 8	106	24
9 - 12	136	31
13 or more	79	18

It is not surprising that group homes averaged the greatest number of residents (12) and that these homes were also most likely to include professional staff. In fact, the average group home had three staff and nine retarded residents. Table IV.4 also shows that semi-independent settings averaged eight persons, but that average refers to the number of persons living semi-independently in one supervised setting. Such settings usually consisted of a number of apartments supervised by a staff (generally a staff of two persons for six residents.) Foster homes were surprisingly large, averaging two parents and five other residents.

TABLE IV.4
AVERAGE NUMBER OF RESIDENTS BY SETTING

Setting	Average No. of Residents
Natural homes	5
Foster homes	7
Group homes	12
Semi-independent	8
Independent	1

Although most of the study group members were living with a number of other people, nearly everyone (93 percent) had their own bedrooms. Only 5 percent shared bedrooms with one or two other persons, and the remaining 2 percent shared bedrooms with three or more people. Thus, most of the people had private space available where they lived.

All study group members except those living independently were under some kind of supervision. The characteristics of those in supervisory roles varied considerably and in predictable ways. (See Table IV.5.)

TABLE IV.5
STAFF EDUCATION AND EXPERIENCE

Education and Experience	Natural Home	Foster Home	Group Home	Semi-Independent
Average years of education	11	12	15	15
Most common degree	H.S.	H.S.	B.A.	B.A.
Most common major	—	—	Psychology	Psychology or Education
Average years of experience	19	9	4	4

Group homes tended to be staffed by "house managers" or "house parents" who had B.A.'s in psychology or education. Many had worked as attendants or social workers prior to becoming house parents, and on the average they had four years of experience working with retarded persons. Staff in semi-independent living situations were also likely to have B.A.'s in psychology or education and four years of experience in working with retarded persons. The family heads of foster and natural homes generally had high school educations, but they had an average of 19 years of experience with retarded persons — obviously, many had had retarded children living in their homes. Foster families also had considerable experience — nine years on the average — in working or living with retarded persons.

Physical Characteristics of the Residence*

The physical attributes of the setting — type and condition of buildings — in which retarded people live can also affect residential

---

* This information was based on interviewer observations covering 87 percent of the study group homes. The remainder of the settings were not seen by interviewers and could not be evaluated.

experiences. Over half the study group members lived in single-family dwellings, but the type of dwelling varied by setting. People living semi-independently or independently tended to live in multifamily buildings, with only 9 out of 40 semi-independent and 8 out of 46 independent persons living in single-family settings. Most of the semi-independent and independent persons lived in apartments located in buildings containing units for two or more families. Very few persons (1 percent) lived in rooming houses or mobile homes. (See Appendix C, Table C.1.) Based on these data, it appears that the study group members were located in dwellings which were in keeping with the concept of a private or family residence.

The houses in which the mentally retarded people lived were generally well-maintained, clean, and homelike. (See Appendix C, Tables C.2, C.3, and C.4.) The interiors of most dwellings were rated as either in excellent or moderate condition*(61 and 33 percent, respectively), with only 6 percent in poor condition. Similarly, the great majority of houses (89 percent) were rated as very clean or reasonably clean, while only 11 percent were rated as dirty and not well kept.

The overwhelming proportion of dwellings (93 percent) were also considered to be extremely homelike.** Only 7 percent were rated as moderately homelike because they gave some evidence of an institutional atmosphere (e.g., lack of pictures on the wall, few personal touches, and highly structured patterns of activity). Only one residence, a group home, was rated as low in homelike qualities because of its strong institutional qualities. Based on these judgments, the study group members appeared to live in relatively homelike dwellings.

Relationship of the Residence to the Community

Acceptance of the concept of normalization for retarded persons has led to increased emphasis on the importance of locating them in typical residential neighborhoods. In general, it appears that the study group members had the opportunity to live in such neighborhoods. Only 5 percent were located in homes on streets that were primarily commercial or industrial, while almost two-thirds lived on completely residential streets.

---

* Condition was rated by the interviewer on a three-point scale: "excellent condition" meant that the residence was in excellent repair and attractively decorated; "moderate condition" meant it was well-kept, but in need of minor repairs, and "poor condition" meant it was obviously in need of major repairs (e.g., peeling paint and other indications of being run-down).

** "Homelike atmosphere" referred to comfortable furnishings, availability of personal space, allowance for personal possessions, and a homelike rhythm and feeling in the house.

TABLE IV.6
TYPE OF STREET

Street Type	N(376)	%
Residential	234	62
Mixed	47	12
Commercial	15	4
Industrial	2	1
Rural	38	10
Unknown	40	11

Group, semi-independent, and independent residences were likely to be located in urban areas, less than half a mile from some type of shopping area, while natural and foster homes were more likely to be outside of urban centers and a mile or further from shopping districts. In keeping with these differences, more than half of the group, semi-independent, and independent residences were located within half a mile of public transportation, while natural and foster family residences were further removed. (See Appendix C, Tables C.5, C.6, and C.7.) It should be noted, however, that more than one-third of the group homes and semi-independent residences were located in areas where no public transportation was available. Since only four study group members had drivers' licenses, most people were dependent on others for transportation.

Friendliness of the Community

Family members of the retarded persons were asked to evaluate community friendliness. About three-fourths of the respondents felt that the community was friendly while only 4 percent felt it was definitely unfriendly. There were substantial differences according to age of study group members: 95 percent of the families of children felt the community they lived in was friendly, but only 42 percent of those representing adults were as positive and 20 percent felt that the communities in which adults lived were unfriendly. Although these responses perhaps reflect a tendency for communities to be more friendly toward retarded children than retarded adults (see Table IV.7), it is significant that one-fifth of the families of adults also saw the community as unfriendly.

Perceptions of the friendliness of the community and neighborhood are also related to the level of retardation. (See Table IV.8.)

TABLE IV.7
FAMILY PERCEPTIONS OF COMMUNITY FRIENDLINESS
BY AGE

Friendliness	Children		Adults	
	N(75)	%	N(290)	%
Very friendly	51	68	93	32
Friendly	20	26	28	10
Neutral	2	3	111	38
Unfriendly	2	3	37	13
Very unfriendly	—	—	21	7

TABLE IV.8
FAMILY PERCEPTIONS OF COMMUNITY FRIENDLINESS
BY LEVEL OF RETARDATION

Friendliness	Level of Retardation					
	Mild		Moderate		Severe	
	N(136)	%	N(117)	%	N(97)	%
Very friendly	40	31	46	39	50	52
Friendly	12	9	11	10	3	3
Neutral	56	43	33	28	33	34
Un-friendly	17	13	14	12	6	6
Very un-friendly	5	4	13	11	5	5

The families of mildly retarded people were least likely to see the community as friendly (only 40 percent), while those speaking for the severely retarded were most likely to characterize it as friendly. The families of mildly and moderately retarded persons were most likely to label their communities as unfriendly (17 and 23 percent, respectively), as compared with only 11 percent of the families of severely retarded persons. Considering the large proportion of families who felt the community was unfriendly or neutral, efforts should perhaps be directed at improving community attitudes toward retarded people. This finding is corrobarated by the fact that 20 percent of the families felt that the community's lack of acceptance of the study group member posed a problem for them. Certainly, the challenge of developing a more normal life should be met not only by the retarded, but by the community as well. However, it is doubtful that community attitudes will be changed without careful planning and programs designed to educate people in regard to this responsibility.

RESIDENTIAL EXPERIENCES

Beyond the objective characteristics of the residence, of course, the subjective perceptions of mentally retarded individuals and their families about living together play a crucial role in the overall community experiences of mentally retarded people. Study group members gave generally favorable reports of their residential experiences in the community. They liked where they were living, felt that they were adjusting well to their new surroundings, and did not report many problems at home. These perceptions were largely corroborated by the families of the residents.

Study Group Perceptions of Residential Experiences

The study group members were satisfied with their current homes. (See Appendix C, Tables C.8 and C.9.) Only about 10 percent of the people said they did not like where they were living. These responses are remarkably similar to those reported in the 1975 census for the U.S. population as a whole, in which 8.2 percent of the population indicated dissatisfaction with place of residence.[1] Thus, retarded people are apparently about as likely as nonretarded people to be satisfied with their homes.

Although most people responded that they liked where they were currently living, about one-third indicated they would rather live elsewhere. (See Figure IV.1 for examples of their comments.) The most frequently mentioned preferred residences were apartments or homes of their own (40 percent), or the homes of natural families (36 percent). Only four individuals indicated that they would prefer to live in an institution. When study group members were asked if they would prefer to live in the community or in the institution, a total of 37 people — 21 of whom had already returned to live in an institution — said they preferred living in the institution.

FIGURE IV.1
RESIDENTIAL PREFERENCES

Where would you rather live?

I would like to live in an apartment with another girl.

An apartment house someday with a boy.

Might later on have my own house — right in the middle of town. That way you don't have to walk your legs off. Boy, they make a lot of new houses out here.

An apartment closer to work.

At hostel — big step — be on my own. Go more places, do things. That's a big step coming up. Have tennis courts, basketball, swimming pool. Cook for self.

I'd rather live on my own — or in hostel — like apartment houses with counselors. swimming, trips, activities with counselors, buy their own food. Two in a room.

In an apartment with somebody else where I can work and take care of myself. Can't do it now, but soon I hope to.

Would you rather live where you are now or at the institution?

I'd rather live at the institution. Anybody give me that choice I'll take it. Guess I got a release so I can't go back. They told me if I break 16 rules I can go back, so I broke 16 rules and I still can't go back. They should have turned me loose when I was 23 years old instead of at 35 years old. Now you get so used to a place you want to go back to the place.

I don't like the institution — too much rules. You know what rules are? You can't do what you want. They check your pockets — they look for money. I'm glad I'm not down there anymore.

The vast majority of the people liked where they were living and preferred it to other options. To explore the matter further, we asked them to give examples both of what they did and did not like about their current residence. Selected responses are listed in Figures IV.2 and IV.3, respectively.

FIGURE IV.2
LIKES ABOUT THE RESIDENCE

I like living in an apartment. More freedom — go shopping, go down-town, go to movies. We go places. The apartment is pretty.

Nice and quiet. Nice and clean. Like a home.

Cleaning up the house and stuff. There ain't no trouble, you know. You can get along with people, you go shopping with others, you learn how to pay your own rent so when you're on your own, you'll know.

I like my foster mother. I have my own room, color TV, bicycle.

They treat me nice — all the food I want — we go a lot of places — sing in choir. Get allowance, clean room, take out garbage, help grand-ma do many kinds of chores.

Well, you can cook own breakfast, and then go out to work and I be on my own, I go up to my room and watch TV.

I love it here. I love my dad. My dad died and sold his house. I love the farm here. I love my foster parents — my grandpa is gone. I love my girlfriend A; she reminds me of my mother . . . . I like to take care of the puppies, kittens, and cows. I like to grow flowers, gardens; like to pull weeds in gardens, to can. Like to can ketchup . . . I have a calf to water . . . . Sometimes I make coffee. A makes me coffee. We make our own breakfast and supper . . . . . I love my family doctor.

Having a roof over our heads, being able to go places without being stuck in the home, some of the girls, especially M and S, and my roommate. My boy friend. Hope to be out on my own — not by my-self either.

We got a brand new home now. I like to make the beds, and clean off the furniture and I like to go to my own church. I got my own preacher. I like to see my brother.

Cook myself; clean up apartment. Go by myself without others tag-ging along. Stay up late. Keeps me out of trouble.

FIGURE IV.3
DISLIKES ABOUT THE RESIDENCE

It's too small of a town. I prefer living in bigger town. Small town people watch you too close and big towns don't. Have more stores in big town. Small town don't.

The husband was mean. Wanted to throw a chair when I wouldn't go to bed. Didn't take us to church, didn't go anywhere, but shopping. I always had to work — work for other resident and myself. Foster mother complained that I wouldn't confide in her. I like to stay to myself. She liked J more than me 'cause J talked to her. Never fed us lunch, just breakfast and dinner. Couldn't sit in living room or touch dog. The parents would never eat with us. Supposed to be members of family but didn't treat us like one — leftovers. Couldn't sleep late, had to get up even on Saturday. Sunday didn't do anything all day. J went to summer camp; I didn't. Husband wanted her to take care of J. I have seizures so I can't do that. I liked the lady but not husband. Had to be quiet so not to wake him.

There was one person I didn't like He was always bothering the girls — coming to their rooms at night and asking them if they would do something dirty. And he would come to my room and ask me to do something dirty. I always told him no. And then he went and told his wife that I wanted to make babies with him. So she went and called up the school here.

The most frequently mentioned aspect of residential living concerned relationships with other people in the home. (See Table IV.9.) Almost half the study group members said they liked some of the people, while more than 80 percent said they didn't like some of the people with whom they were living. The next most commonly noted aspect was the extent of freedom or independence, with almost a quarter of the group mentioning this as something they liked about living in the community. Almost as many felt that social or recreational activities were important features of their residence. Other aspects were considerably less important, or at least were less likely to be mentioned by the study group members.

The importance which the study group members placed on getting along with the people with whom they were living is not particularly surprising, since most of us prefer to live with people we like. The difference is that the retarded people may have had less to say about who their housemates would be. The fact that they lived with a relatively large number of other people may well be a factor in their

TABLE IV.9
LIKES AND DISLIKES ABOUT RESIDENCE

	Like		Dislike	
	N [a]	%	N [a]	%
Other people living there	200	45	347	81
Degree of freedom and independence	102	23	39	7
Extent of social or recreational activities	96	22	10	2
Opportunities to learn	60	14	1	1
Physical environment	55	13	10	2
Extent of privacy	43	10	11	3
Food	31	7	3	1
Extent of peace and quiet	17	4	11	3

[a] Numbers and percentages refer to the total number and percent of times an attribute was mentioned.

frequent comments on other residents. But whatever the family size, more emphasis should perhaps be placed on evaluating the social compatibility of retarded people who are placed together in residences.

Perceptions of Adjustment to the Residence

We were greatly concerned with determining the extent to which the retarded people were adjusting to their new residences in the community. Both the families and the retarded people whom we questioned viewed adjustment favorably, in terms of both the residential setting and the other residents. (See Appendix C, Tables C.10, C.11, C.12 and C.13.) There were few differences among responses by families of adults and those of children concerning adaptation to the new living situation. Over 90 percent of both groups indicated that there were no difficulties in adjusting to the house. Children were seen as somewhat more likely to have problems relating to other residents (13 percent) than adults (10 percent). Most impressive, however, is the large proportion of people who were perceived as adapting well. (See Appendix C, Table C.10.)

Level of retardation did not seem to influence adaptation to the home or residents in the home. Again, no more than 10 percent of the people at all levels of retardation were reported by their families to be making a poor adjustment. Slightly more of the moderately retarded were seen as having trouble adjusting to the house (13 percent), while 11 percent of the mildly retarded had difficulty adjusting to other people in the residence. (See Appendix C, Table C.13.)

When the residents themselves were asked about their adjustment to the house and other residents, their evaluations were as positive as those of their families. Only 5 percent of the children and 9 percent of the adults perceived their adjustment to the house as poor. Children were somewhat more likely to see relationships with other residents as poor (14 and 8 percent, respectively). Level of retardation made some difference, in that the severely retarded were least likely to report a poor adjustment to either the house or other residents, but the overwhelming fact is that very few of the residents perceived real problems with adjustment. (See Appendix C, Table C.11 and C.12.)

Other indicators of residential adjustment point to the presence of some problems. For example, over half the families felt that discipline was at least somewhat of a problem. (See Table IX.3, p. 132.) More than one-third of the families indicated that stress on family relationships was at least somewhat of a problem, and lack of temporary relief was a problem reported by about one-fifth of the families. Similarly, over half the families felt that family relationships were at least somewhat of a problem. (See Table IX.1, p.129.) The study group members themselves were somewhat less likely to perceive family relationships as a problem, with almost 60 percent feeling that they posed no problems at all for them. (See Table IX.2,p. 130.)

In general, then, although most of the families and study group members felt that the latter were adjusting well to the home, many families nevertheless noted specific problems in having the retarded person in the home.

Availability of Alternative Residences

We asked the families whether they felt other residences were available for the retarded people, and whether those available were more or less supervised than the current residence. (See Table IV.10.) Of those indicating that other residences were available, 34 percent felt they were less supervised whereas 45 percent characterized them as more supervised. Less than half of the families felt that other housing, either more or less supervised, was available. While it is difficult to estimate how accurate these perceptions are, the responses suggest that a large number of those families responsible for retarded people feel that residential alternatives are somewhat limited.

TABLE IV.10
FAMILY PERCEPTIONS OF THE
AVAILABILITY OF ALTERNATIVE RESIDENCES

	Available		Not Available		Uncertain		Total
	N	%	N	%	N	%	
More supervised	151	34	281	64	8	2	440
Less supervised	197	45	164	37	79	18	440

PREVIOUS RESIDENTIAL EXPERIENCES

Study group members were interviewed from six months to three and a half years from the time of their initial placement in the community. On the average, persons had been living in the community for two years and three months at the time of the study. During this period, approximately one-third of the group moved at least once, with a subsequent redistribution in the proportion of persons living in different types of settings. (See Table IV.11.)

TABLE IV.11
RESIDENTIAL PLACEMENTS:
INITIAL, CURRENT, ONE YEAR HENCE

Setting	Initial		Current		One Year Hence	
	N(440)	%	N(440)	%	N(383)	%
Natural parent	56	13	61	14	49	13
Foster parent	63	14	78	18	61	16
Group home	290	66	209	47	153	40
Semi-independent	26	6	45	10	58	15
Independent	5	1	47	11	62	16

Upon release, two-thirds of the people had moved to group homes while only 7 percent had gone to live in semi-independent or independent settings. At the time of the study, however, less than half the people were living in group homes, and the number of people living independently or semi-independently had increased to 21 percent. When asked to project the living situation one year hence (i.e., a year after the interview was conducted), only 35 percent predicted that study group members would be in group homes, and 27 percent foresaw semi-independent or independent arrangements. It seems that about 14 percent of the total study group moved into more independent or less structured and supervised settings during the approximately two years following release and another 6 percent were expected to move in the next year.

The tendency to move into more independent settings requiring greater skills in self-maintenance was reinforced when we examined movement patterns by age, level of retardation, and reasons for moving. Children were less likely to move than adults, and severely and moderately retarded people were less likely to move than mildly retarded people. (See Tables IV.12 and IV.13.) It appears that people with more advanced skills were more likely to move than those with fewer or less advanced skills.

TABLE IV.12
NUMBER OF SETTINGS LIVED IN BY AGE

Number of Settings	Children		Adults		Total	
	N(83)	%	N(357)	%	N(440)	%
One	60	72	233	65	293	67
Two	17	21	60	17	77	18
Three	5	6	35	10	40	9
Four or more	1	1	29	8	30	6

TABLE IV.13
NUMBER OF SETTINGS LIVED IN BY LEVEL OF RETARDATION

Number of Settings	Level of Retardation							
	Mild		Moderate		Severe		Total	
	N(171)	%	N(137)	%	N(106)	%	N(414)	%
One	103	60	99	72	75	70	277	67
Two	31	18	17	12	22	21	70	17
Three	25	15	8	6	5	5	38	9
Four or more	12	7	13	10	4	4	29	7

The reasons for moving further substantiate this line of argument. (See Table IV.14.) About one-quarter of the moves were made because the expected time of stay had expired; in effect, the resident had "completed" the program — that is, the age, time, or skill requirements of the residence. Another quarter moved simply because they wanted to and another quarter because their families, guardians, or others responsible for them felt it best if they moved. Only 12 percent of the moves took place because the other residents no longer wanted them living there.

TABLE IV.14
REASONS FOR MOVING

Reasons	N(271)	%
Resident wanted to move	73	27
Others[a] wanted resident to move	66	24
Expected time of stay expired	61	23
Residence was closed	32	12
Other residents wanted resident to move	33	12
Resident left area	6	2

[a] Family, guardian, or another individual responsible for resident.

SUMMARY

Even though the study group members had been living in the community for a relatively brief period of time (on the average, a little more than two years), several important trends emerged from the data.

Study group members were living in residences which were adequate in terms of their physical conditions. Most lived in a clean and homelike atmosphere. Most people were living in residential as opposed to commercial or industrial areas, and were relatively close to shopping areas. However, more than one-third of the study group had no access to public transportation.

Although the homes were generally "normal" in terms of atmosphere and location, family size tended to be considerably larger than the average for the United States. Only about one-quarter of the study group lived in homes with four or fewer people; the average home consisted of eight people. National statistics indicate that in 1976 only 3.4 percent of the United States population lived in households containing seven or more people and that 83 percent live in households containing four or fewer.[2] It is difficult to judge whether large family size is detrimental to residential adjustment, but if the goal is to establish more normal environments for retarded persons, increased attention should be given to household size.

The data from the national survey conducted as part of the study indicate that while the most common community placement is the natural family, most mentally retarded people are released into homes which are neither "true" families nor known to the retarded person prior to institutionalization. Thus, most retarded people are released into environments created specifically to accommodate deinstitutionalized mentally retarded people. In the study group the most common placements were group homes, followed by foster homes, and then natural families, with semi-independent and independent living settings least common.

Following release from the institution, there is a tendency for retarded people to move gradually into more independent settings. Approximately 7 percent of the study group members had expected to move into a different type of setting, generally one which would be less supervised during the next year. The most common move was from group homes to semi-independent and independent living situations.   This particular pattern may be explained by the fact that "staffed" homes tend to be part of a structured network of residential alternatives, unlike natural or foster homes.

Fewer than half the families reported the existence of less supervised residences available within the community, and slightly more than one-third indicated that more supervised residences were available. Thus, although some movement was apparent among study group members, it is quite possible that there would have been greater mobility if more residential alternatives had existed.

The communities in which study group members lived were generally seen as friendly toward the retarded people, although about one-fifth of the study group lived in communities which were not perceived as supportive. Most of the study group members felt they were making a good adjustment to their homes and to the people with whom they were living; families corroborated this view. However, more than one-third of the families felt that stress on family relations presented at least somewhat of a problem for them. Most of the study group liked where they were living, and the overwhelming majority preferred living in the community to living at the institution.

REFERENCES

1. *Social Indicators, 1976: Selected Data on Social Conditions and Trends in the United States* (Washington, D.C.: U.S. Department of Commerce, Office of Federal Statistics Policy and Standards, Bureau of the Census, December 1977).

2. *Social Indicators, 1976.*

Chapter V
What Are They Doing:
Work and School Placements

> The day activity of mentally retarded people is the most critical component of their community adjustment . . . . They drastically and poignantly want to be productive, useful, wage-earning members of society . . . .
>
> —(comment by a house manager)

In this chapter we describe the characteristics of the study group members' daytime activities, as well as their satisfaction with these day placements and the problems encountered in them. The term "day placement" refers to the jobs, programs, or training activities in which study group members were involved on a regular basis, usually outside of their residence.

Information was gathered from members of the study group and their families about three major day placement categories — work, schools, and day activity centers. Day placements are generally arranged by institutional or community staff prior to the individual's release into the community. In fact, almost all of the institutions which we contacted indicated that the availability of a day placement was one of the primary criteria which they used to determine whether an individual should be released to the community.

Because work and school are essential aspects of community living and independent functioning for all people, day placements are a vital component of the lives of persons released from institutions into community settings. Involvement in day activities is often considered by human service professionals as one of the keys to normalized living. In addition, day placements frequently provide critical services and training to people, as we discuss in Chapters VII and VIII.

Most study group members were participating in some activity during the day, with about 90 percent engaged in a formal activity at the time of the interview. (See Table V.1.) About one-third of the people were involved in more than one activity, usually a work placement and a school program. Among the people we studied there was a considerable range in the type of day activities. Slightly over half of them worked, either in "competitive" jobs in the labor market or in sheltered jobs or workshops. Forty percent were in either day or night school, while about one-quarter of the group were currently attending day activity center-programs other than work or school which offer training or special activities on a regular basis. On the average, they spent about 30 hours a week in these activities.

There were some interesting differences among the day placements according to age and level of retardation. (See Tables V.2 and V.3.) As could be expected, children were involved primarily in school placements (79 percent), whereas adults were most frequently working at jobs (66 percent). The most notable difference according to level of retardation was that mildly retarded persons were placed most frequently in jobs (70 percent) and least frequently in day activity centers (19 percent). Conversely, jobs were the least common kind of placement for severely retarded persons (37 percent) and day activities were most common (44 percent). These patterns are very similar to the study group members' participation in day placements while institutionalized (see Chapter III).

TABLE V.1
CURRENT DAY PLACEMENTS[a]

Type of Day Placement	N	%
Job (competitive or sheltered employment)	247	55
School (attend classes in day or night)	178	40
Special day activity center or program	124	28
No school, work, or day activity program	49	11

[a] In Tables V.1, V.2, and V.3, percentages do not equal 100 percent because some persons participated in more than one type of day placement.

TABLE V.2
CURRENT DAY PLACEMENTS BY AGE

Type of Day Placement	Children		Adults	
	N	%	N	%
Job (competitive or sheltered employment)	8	9	237	66
School (attend classes in day or night)	67	79	109	30
Special day activity center or program	16	19	107	30
No school, work, or day activity program	8	9	39	11

TABLE V.3
CURRENT DAY PLACEMENTS BY LEVEL OF RETARDATION

| Type of Day Placement | Level of Retardation | | | | | |
| | Mild | | Moderate | | Severe | |
	N	%	N	%	N	%
Job (competitive or sheltered employment)	119	70	77	56	39	37
School (attend classes in day or night)	52	30	50	43	45	42
Special day activity center or program	32	19	37	27	44	44
No school, work, or day activity program	18	11	17	12	9	9

Although the data show that most persons were involved in day placements, 11 percent were not involved in any day placement at the time the interviews were conducted. However, about half of this group had participated in a day placement(s) at some time since release from the institution. This means that less than 5 percent of the study group had *never* been in a day placement in the community. When family respondents were asked why the individual was not currently in a day placement, the most frequently cited reason was that there were no appropriate placements in the community. In many other cases, the individual was reluctant or did not want to participate, or was dropped from the program because he or she was unable to keep up with its demands. The lack of day placements was a serious problem for the study group members and their families. The gravity of these situations is emphasized in some of the interviewers' notes:

> Mary sees neighbors, relatives, goes to swimming area, but *no* day activity program since released. Also confined to wheelchair. She could be in some day activity except she cannot toilet for herself.

> Very satisfied parent and daughter except for lack of a day program and chance to meet others more often. Has been without a day program for two years due to lack of transportation.

> Unfortunately, Larry was refused for the Program (according to social worker, this behavior mod program would be great for Larry) because he is "too old," "may be destructive." It seems a general rule that there are not enough appropriate settings (in some places, none) in communities for certain people like Larry.

The day placement histories of the study group members who participated in day programs were quite stable. Almost two-thirds of the people had remained in the same day placement since they were released from the institution. Those who had changed programs usually had left the first because they had completed it (i.e., reached the age, skill, or time limits of the program) or had not wanted to stay in it. In most cases, the reasons for leaving placements was *not* an inability to adjust to a program or to cope with the activities.

In an effort to determine what families expected of study group members in the future, we asked family respondents what type of day placement they thought the individual would be involved in one year from the time of the interview. Almost two-thirds of the families said that the individual would probably be in the current day activity program.

WORK PLACEMENTS

> Dennis was unusual because he was the first person I spoke to who would have preferred to go back to the institution. He said the reason for that was that at the institution he had a job working in the laundry. In the community he just worked in a sheltered workshop which did not give him a feeling of satisfaction.
>   (comment by an interviewer about a study group member)

Work was the most common day activity among study group members. Of the 247 persons who were involved in work placements, three-quarters of them were in sheltered work situations, such as sheltered workshops, rehabilitation centers, or job training centers. The remaining one-quarter worked in competitive employment situations.   (See Table V.4.) The proportion of persons in sheltered and regular employment differed greatly by level of retardation. Of the

TABLE V.4
TYPE OF WORK PLACEMENT

Type of Work Placement	N(247)	%
Competitive job (regular employment)	62	25
Sheltered job (sheltered workshop, rehabilitation center, or job training center)	185	75

severely retarded persons in job placements, only 5 percent worked at regular jobs and 95 percent worked in sheltered situations, whereas 30 percent of the mildly retarded and 24 percent of the moderately retarded persons worked in regular employment situations. (See Table V.5.)

TABLE V.5
TYPE OF WORK PLACEMENT BY LEVEL OF RETARDATION

| Type of Work Placement | Level of Retardation | | | | | |
| | Mild | | Moderate | | Severe | |
	N(117)	%	N(76)	%	N(39)	%
Competitive job (regular employment	36	30	18	24	2	5
Sheltered job (sheltered workshop, rehabilitation center, or job training center)	81	70	58	76	37	95

On the average, people spent about 30 hours per week at their jobs. About half of them worked 35 hours or more each week (up to 48 hours per week in one case). Length of employment in these jobs averaged 17 months and ranged from less than one month to six years. About half of the study group members had worked at their jobs for 14 months or longer.

Most of the work which the study group members performed could be classified as unskilled or semiskilled. Many of the competitive jobs entailed janitorial or other maintenance work. In sheltered environments, individuals tended to perform simple assembly, packing, and sorting tasks. The following are some descriptions by study group members of their work:

Maintenance, how to make things look all clean, to keep inside of apartment or house clean. At night, go down to people's offices and clean up. Empty ashtrays, see chairs, floors, and rugs are clean.

Wash dishes and scrub floors.

Make flour, pig feed, and chicken feed, dairy feed; sack the barley feed; deliver feed and haul hay.

Dishwashing.

Pick up garbage.

Clean and all that — on the floor cleaning, part time in kitchen — dishwashing, help serve.

Sort laundry. Help wash laundry. Sweep up laundry.

I'm a busboy. I pick up dishes off the table. Sometimes I help the lady on the dishwasher — empty trash can — sometimes I sweep the sidewalks.

Take cans out first, then take trash out and put clean trash bags in; then sweep floor and mop the floor. Then I'm done.

The types of work or the tasks involved in work placements were extremely important to the retarded people we interviewed and were major factors in their satisfaction or dissatisfaction with their jobs. When asked what they liked or disliked about their work, individuals most frequently cited the type of work they performed. The next most common response concerned the people they worked with and for, followed by the money which they made. (See Figure V.1.)

In general study group members were pleased with their work; almost two-thirds of them expressed satisfaction. Degree of satisfaction decreased somewhat with level of retardation: 67 percent of the mildly retarded individuals but only 58 percent of the severely retarded said they liked their jobs.

FIGURE V.1
WORK LIKES AND DISLIKES

What do you like about your work?

It's hard and makes you tired once in a while. Like to iron the big machine. Like to run the dryers, like sorting even if it is hard, taking towels to rehab unit. John is there and I like that.

Tips. How much I'm making and I like the people there. Like doing rooms.

The people were nice. I liked my boss; I miss it. The job was fun. I liked the coffee breaks. Met new people and talked to them. I liked taking tests.

Work at my school. It's okay. I like the money — get to buy clothes. The work is more important though than the money is. I like the work.

Like people I work with, like my boss, they're very kind, good people. I like the kinds of things I do. They've given me clothes and dresses and things. I really enjoy it.

Like doing dishes, cleaning dish room to cleaning cafe. Mopping and sweeping floors, and also washing and drying towels.

Like being there on time, packing boxes everyday, making money. Nothing else.

Nothing really to like about it except there are some nice girls there.

What do you not like about your work?

If you do wrong — they scold you and holler at you. When we take trips, I can't go with my own friends. They make me go with someone else. They make you play during recreation time when you don't want to play. Some kids are jealous of me because I have friends.

Not enough pay. $5.00 for the week. You can't buy soap, patterns, shampoo. I want to make more money. Sitting too much, I like moving around. Like in a restaurant. Funny hours — 8:30 to 4:00 with many breaks. I don't like the hours. In the winter my money went down. I got a lot of money — unemployment. I'm not working — only do day work a few days in a beauty parlor.

There isn't anything I don't like except sometimes I don't have anything to do and have to wait.

That it's hard — hard being a maid.

The part I don't like is when they move me around. I like being in one place.

No. I don't like fighting. (They don't fight at work, though.) The boss checks us to see if work is done. If I have trouble, I can go to office and the boss straightens it out.

Although most people were satisfied with their jobs, many of their problems in the community were related to work. When family respondents were given a list of problems which could be encountered by mentally retarded persons living in the community and were asked to rate the importance of each problem (big problem, somewhat of a problem, not a problem), finding a job and keeping it were among the most frequently mentioned problems. Finding a job was considered a problem in 43 percent and keeping a job in 39 percent of the cases. When study group members were asked about their problems in the community, 24 percent of them cited finding a job and 11 percent cited keeping a job as problematic.

Given the general economic and employment conditions which prevailed in these communities at the time of the interviews, it is not surprising that finding and keeping jobs often presented problems for study group members. When jobs are scarce for the population at large, unemployment problems are even more severe for mentally retarded persons, who are typically among those "last hired, first fired."

SCHOOL PLACEMENTS

Forty percent of the study group participated in school placements — typically in public school programs. Very few individuals, however, were placed in the "mainstream" of school programs (i.e., in regular classes held in the public schools). Most were in specialized programs — about 40 percent were enrolled in special classes in special schools, and about 26 percent attended special classes in regular schools. Thus, although a large number of persons were involved in school placements, they were not often integrated into regular school programs with students who were not retarded. Severely retarded clients were placed in special programs in special schools more frequently than mildly or moderately retarded members of the study group.

Although most study group members attended school during the day, participation in night classes was also common. Fifty-eight individuals attended regular or special night classes, almost all held in public schools. Those attending night classes were usually involved in other placements during the day, such as jobs, day schools, or day activity centers.

About half of the day school programs were run during the entire year, while half were in operation only during the traditional academic year. Students spent an average of 22 hours a week in day schools (about 40 percent of the day students were in school for 25 hours or more per week). About half of the night school students spent four hours or more per week in their classes. The average length of time which both day and night students had remained in their placements was 17 months. About half of the day students had been enrolled for at least one year, and half of the night school students had attended classes for 17 months or more.

Study group members were more satisfied with their school place-ments than they were with their work placements. Ninety percent of them said they liked the school programs in which they were involved (compared to 63 percent of the group who were satisfied with their work placements). Severely retarded members of the group were more satisfied with their school placements than the mildly or moderately retarded students. Ninety-seven percent of the severely retarded stu-dents said they liked school, whereas 80 percent of the mildly retarded and 92 percent of the moderately retarded expressed satisfaction. The most frequently mentioned reasons for liking school were fun or easy school work, good food, and enjoyable recreational activities. (See Figure V.2.) Unfriendly classmates and difficult or uninteresting school work were most often cited as reasons for disliking school.

FIGURE V.2
SCHOOL LIKES

What do you like about school?

Math, English, arithmetic. I like all the things I do there. Like to dance, play basketball and softball, and jump on trampoline once in a while.

Learn new things, new skills. Love to read. Like some math. Our teacher, breaks.

Teacher writing numbers and such, have films and stuff. Got friends to talk to. The teacher there — trying to help you with your numbers and stuff. Sometimes I have treats and stuff. Cookies and stuff. Do fine.

Learn something. Read. Be good. Had a show there about Washington, D.C. Count numbers — work on maps. Learn how to put address on it.

Gym, basketball games I'm in, hiking, taking bus, going with Carol, writing, football, sports. That's all.

I'll be graduating soon. Like taking up sewing. Know how to pin material. I got friends there. Lot of kids. I like to learn.

Teacher, my work, I was going to two schools. They were teaching me to go to R. High. I had special classes, I had shop and gym, I liked the principal and I had a girlfriend. I'd meet different kinds at the school. School wasn't too far from my home.

I like it all. I like education; it helps you get out of the house.

DAY ACTIVITY PROGRAMS

Twenty-eight percent of the study group members were involved in day activity centers or programs, which usually offered domestic or practical work, prevocational training, or social and recreational activities. People spent an average of 27 hours per week in these placements and had been involved in them for an average of 18 months; half of the day activity participants had been in their programs for 17 months or more.

As we noted in regard to satisfaction with school placements, most of the people (92 percent) liked their day activity programs, with a greater number of severely retarded than mildly or moderately retarded individuals expressing satisfaction. The most frequently mentioned reasons for liking the day activity program were that the activities were fun and interesting and that the participants were nice. As one study group member described his program, *"Everyday play games, go outside, clap your hands, people, play games, count money, it's okay."* Dissatisfaction was most commonly attributed to boring or difficult activities.

OVERALL DAY PLACEMENT ADJUSTMENT

In general, study group members appeared to be actively involved in and satisfied with their day placements. Although the majority expressed satisfaction with their specific placements, when asked if there were something else they would rather do during the day, about half of them responded in the affirmative. Most frequently, they would have preferred competitive employment (about 60 percent of the responses), as indicated in the following comments by study group members:

I would like to carry on a regular job, but I guess there aren't any available, so I'll have to stick with this. Nothing else.

I'd like a babysitting job. I like kids.

Take care of little kids.

Someday, work in a restaurant — make sodas — wear a uniform.

I'd like to work in laundromat. I like to fold clothes. Steady job — make more money.

I wish I could be a singer like Gladys Knight and the Pips.

I'd rather have a job and make some money.

Overall, both the study group members and their families appeared to be satisfied with the adjustment to day placement. When families were asked to rate adjustment, in terms of work/school relationships on a three-point scale, about two-thirds of the respondents indicated that the individual had adjusted "very well" and an additional 27 percent rated adjustment as "all right." (See Table V.6.) Only 6 percent of the respondents rated adjustment as poor ("not very well"). When study group members were asked to rate themselves on this dimension, their ratings were identical to those of the family respondents.

Families of severely retarded individuals were more satisfied with their adjustment to work and school relationships than were the families of mildly and moderately retarded members of the study group. Seventy-two percent of the families of severely retarded persons indicated that they were adjusting "very well," whereas this high rating was given by only 61 percent of the families of mildly retarded individuals and by 67 percent of the families of moderately retarded persons. (See Table V.7.) Similarly, only 2 percent of the families of

TABLE V.6
FAMILY PERCEPTION OF STUDY GROUP'S ADJUSTMENT TO WORK/SCHOOL RELATIONSHIPS

Adjustment Ratings	N(412)	%
Very well	276	67
All right	112	27
Not very well	24	6

TABLE V.7
FAMILY PERCEPTION OF STUDY GROUP'S ADJUSTMENT TO WORK/SCHOOL RELATIONSHIPS BY LEVEL OF RETARDATION

Adjustment Ratings	Level of Retardation					
	Mild		Moderate		Severe	
	N(153)	%	N(124)	%	N(94)	%
Very well	98	61	83	67	68	72
All right	52	32	30	24	24	26
Not very well	3	7	11	9	2	2

severely retarded persons indicated that they were *not* doing very well, as opposed to 9 percent of the families of moderately retarded and 7 percent of the families of mildly retarded persons.

These differences in adjustment ratings according to level of retardation are difficult to interpret. Are the severely retarded persons adjusting more easily to the community than the less severely handicapped, or might this variance be the result of different sets of expectations? Is satisfaction with the adjustment of severely retarded individuals so high because families have low expectations of these people's abilities?

Note, too, that the severely retarded individuals expressed greater satisfaction with their school and day activity center placements than did those who were less retarded. (However, they were less frequently satisfied with their work placements.) Again, we must question whether these severely retarded persons are more satisfied because of the high quality of their placements or because of their low expectations of these activities and their own participation in them. We raise this question not to downgrade the quality of the placements or the credibility of the data, but because the concept of expectation is so integral to that of community adjustment, and the two are often difficult to disentangle.

SUMMARY

The overwhelming majority of study group members (about 90 percent) were involved in one or more day placements. Slightly over half of them worked, 40 percent were enrolled in school programs, and about one-quarter attended day activity centers. They were generally satisfied with their placements and had remained in these settings for long periods of time. Nonetheless, it appears that many communities did not have adequate choices available, particularly in regard to competitive rather than sheltered employment. As a result, study group members were less satisfied with their work placements than with school or day activity programs or living arrangements. Many expressed the desire to obtain a better job. In fact, a large proportion of the group felt that trying to find adequate employment was one of the biggest problems in living in the community.

Lack of appropriate day placements posed serious problems for those not involved in day programs (11 percent of the group). According to many interviewers, because appropriate placements were lacking in the community, many study group members could not become fully integrated into the community, nor could they develop positive images about themselves and their ability to participate in the mainstream of society. In general, people left day programs because they had completed them and not because of poor adjustment to the placements or unwillingness to participate in them. Thus, it seems evident that more attention needs to be paid to locating productive work opportunities for retarded people living in the community.

Chapter VI
What Are They Doing: Leisure and Social Activities

> The social worker feels he is adjusting beautifully to living on his own. He calls him on occasion to see if he needs any help. The only area the social worker says he needs help with is budgeting and managing his money. However, the resident himself would like more contact with friends to whom he can turn for help. He feels very much alone, he said; has no friends, no one to talk to, and no one to tell his problems to. I felt sorry for him because being competitively employed and living completely independently he had no communication with other residents on his own level of functioning.
>
> (interviewer's remarks about a study group member)

In this chapter we describe several aspects of the study group members social experiences, including their leisure or spare-time activities, and their friendships and other interpersonal relationships. Information on leisure activities and social relationships is essential to an understanding of the community experiences of deinstitutionalized mentally retarded persons. Earlier studies of community adjustment have generally neglected this dimension and focused instead on more measurable factors, such as academic or vocational performance, economic self-sufficiency, or recidivism rate. Although less tangible, the social dimension is vital. Too many individuals are economically self-sufficient, or are performing well in academic programs, but continue to live in social isolation. Apart from participation in structured work or school settings, they may be lost and lonely — without friends, activities, or social outlets. We attempted to explore the social dimension in order to find out how study group members managed in their leisure activities, friendships, and social relationships.

We gathered information on these topics by interviewing both the mentally retarded persons and their families. In many cases, particularly sensitive questions were difficult to ask of study group members, especially those living independently in the community. The questions about friendships and romantic relationships were most problematic — terms such as "close friend" or "relationship" with the opposite sex were difficult to define. One respondent's understanding of these terms might have differed greatly from another's. And even assuming that these terms were clearly understood, it was often difficult for them to discuss these issues with interviewers — the topics were too personal or emotional in many cases. The reader should bear these problems in mind when interpreting the data presented in this chapter.

LEISURE ACTIVITIES

> Violet does leather craft, crochets, paints (not so much anymore because of her arthritis, she said). She enjoys table games such as Monopoly and is a good hair dresser. She also likes "her men, her booze, and her independence" (was thrown into jail one night for intoxication).

We obtained information from families about twelve different types of leisure activities in which study group members participated. The single most common activity was watching TV or listening to the radio, which virtually all people did at least once a week. (See Tables VI.1 and VI.2, which show the extent and frequency of participation in spare-time activities.) Over 80 percent of the study group went shopping, saw movies, and went on vacations during the year preceding the interview. More than two-thirds of the study group went to parties, attended religious activities, visited friends, and participated in sports. The least common activities were dating and attending club or organization meetings.

At least half the study group watched television, went shopping, worked on hobbies, played sports, and attended religious events at least weekly. This represents a reasonable mix of activities in the home, structured activities with groups, and exposure to community activities. In contrast, only 27 percent of the study group members indicated that they go on dates.

Participation in spare-time activities was related to level of retardation, with more severely retarded individuals tending to participate in fewer activities. This was most marked in four activities: going shopping, going to the movies, having hobbies, and going on dates. (See Appendix D, Table D.1.) In general, children participated in fewer leisure activities than did adults — most notably in the following activities: shopping, going to the movies, going to parties, visiting

TABLE VI.1
PARTICIPATION IN LEISURE ACTIVITIES

Type of Activity	Participates		Does Not Participate	
	N	%	N	%
Watching TV, listening to radio	431	98	9	2
Shopping or errands	374	85	66	15
Movies	365	83	75	17
Vacations	356	81	83	19
Parties	330	75	110	25
Religious activities	312	71	127	29
Visiting friends	317	72	123	28
Playing sports	308	70	132	30
Hobbies	277	63	163	37
Attending sports events	255	58	185	42
Going on dates[a]	119	27	299	73
Attending club meetings	84	19	356	81

[a] Asked only about individuals over age 12.

friends, working on hobbies, dating, and attending club meetings. (See Appendix D, Table D.2.) The lower participation rate of children is not surprising since many of these activities are geared toward adult interests or require independent (or adult) transportation.

Despite the fact that many study group members participated frequently in a variety of spare-time activities, many families were not satisfied with the opportunities available in the community. About one-third of the family respondents felt that finding leisure and recreational activities for study group members was a problem, and 10 percent considered it a big problem. Finding leisure activities was considered to be more of a problem by families of adults than by families of children, even though children participated less frequently than adults. This may reflect the fact that families expect adults to be more active than children in spare-time activities outside the home.

ACTIVITIES ALLOWED IN HOMES

In an effort to understand more fully the leisure patterns of the study group, we tried to find out what activities were allowed in the homes. If a person lives in a very restrictive environment, opportunities

TABLE VI.2
FREQUENCY OF PARTICIPATION IN LEISURE ACTIVITIES

Type of Activity	Frequency of Participation								Total
	Does Not Participate		Once a Week		Once a Month		Once a Year or Less		
	N	%	N	%	N	%	N	%	N
Watching TV, listening to radio	9	2	427	97	4	1	—	—	440
Shopping or errands	66	15	312	71	58	13	4	1	440
Movies	75	17	97	22	202	46	66	15	440
Vacations	83	19	10	2	70	16	276	63	439
Parties	110	25	44	10	180	42	101	23	435
Religious activities	127	29	219	50	62	14	31	7	439
Visiting friends	123	28	141	32	114	26	62	14	440
Playing sports	132	30	242	55	48	11	18	4	440
Hobbies	163	37	247	56	26	6	4	1	440
Attending sports events	185	42	48	11	119	27	88	20	440
Going on dates[a]	299	73	42	10	48	12	21	5	410
Attending club meetings	356	81	35	8	40	9	9	2	440

[a] Asked only about individuals over age 12.

to participate in spare-time activities are probably limited. Conversely, if the individual is permitted or encouraged to engage in independent activities in the home, participation is likely to be more frequent.

The data on activities permitted in the home are presented in Table VI.3 which shows the frequency of such activities, broken down by type of residential setting. Over three-quarters of the group were allowed to have guests over for dinner, wear hair and clothing styles of their own choice, decide what clothes to purchase, and decide how to spend their own money. More activities were allowed in group homes and semi-independent settings than in natural/adoptive or foster homes. For example, whereas less than two-thirds of the persons living in natural/adoptive homes were allowed to decide how to spend their own money, about three-quarters of those living in group or semi-independent homes were allowed to make such decisions. People living in natural/adoptive or foster homes were much less likely to come and go at will than those living in semi-independent settings (less than 20 percent, compared to 77 percent). Residents in group or semi-independent settings were also more likely to be able to drink alcoholic beverages, to decide when to make appointments, and to go on dates outside the home than were residents in natural/adoptive or foster homes.

It appears that study group members were typically allowed to participate in activities or make decisions which involved only themselves (e.g., deciding when to go to sleep, wearing hair or clothing style of their own choice, deciding how to spend their own money). However, they tended to be restricted from engaging in activities or making decisions which involved them in social situations (e.g., coming and going at will, having guests overnight, going on dates). This pattern of allowed and restricted activities is consistent with our finding that people were least likely to participate in social activities with friends, particularly outside the home. Given the strong role homes play in recreational and social activities, it is reasonable to assume that participation in these activities was low because they were not allowed or encouraged at home.

As might be expected, children in the study group lived in more restrictive environments than adults. (See Appendix D, Table D.3.) Without exception, a higher proportion of adults than children were allowed to participate in each activity and make decisions. The restrictiveness of the environment also varied greatly according to the level of retardation of the residents. (See Appendix D, Table D.4.) Severely retarded persons lived in more restrictive environments than mildly or moderately retarded individuals. For example, only 20 percent of the severely retarded residents were allowed to come and

TABLE VI.3

ACTIVITIES ALLOWED IN THE HOME BY TYPE OF RESIDENCE

Type of Activity	Natural Home		Foster Home		Group Home		Semi-Indep. Living		Total	
	(N65)	%	N(53)	%	N(188)	%	N(40)	%	N(336)	%
Have guests for dinner	45	82	40	75	166	88	38	95	289	86
Have overnight guests	34	62	27	51	113	60	26	65	200	60
Come and go at will	9	16	7	13	52	28	31	77	99	29
Decide when to go to sleep	32	58	34	64	132	70	36	90	234	70
Wear clothing style of own choice	43	78	45	85	157	83	39	98	284	85
Decide what clothes to purchase	36	65	37	70	149	79	36	90	258	77
Wear hair in own choice of style	41	75	36	68	151	80	38	95	266	79
Decide how to spend own money	33	60	42	79	139	64	31	77	245	73
Go on dates outside of home[a]	16	29	13	24	131	70	35	87	195	58
Drink alcoholic beverages at home[b]	19	35	7	13	60	32	26	65	112	33
Decide when to make appointments[a]	11	20	8	15	105	56	28	70	152	45

[a] Asked only about individuals over age 12.

[b] Asked only about individuals over age 18 or the age of majority in the state.

leave their residence at will, compared to 36 percent of the mildly retarded and 33 percent of the moderately retarded persons. Similar differences are apparent for each of the other activities, and are particularly striking in the cases of buying clothes, spending money, and dating.

A large number of the interviewers' written observations focus on the restrictiveness and overprotection of the homes:

> Mrs. H. seems to drastically restrict G's activities by not allowing him to even try to do things on his own. She admitted that she never even thought of letting him do things for himself because she just doesn't think that he can without getting hurt.

> One rule of the house is that now all TV programs are screened by the houseparents. They take the residents to the library on a regular basis and are encouraged to read rather than watch TV. Interviewer relates story of F mowing the grass with a book in his hand. Houseparents saw this as an indication of how much he was enjoying reading, but F doesn't know how to read and interviewer saw his carrying book around as indication of his pervasive fear of the houseparents rather than love of books.

> Although it was only 8:30, O as well as R (both 25 years old) and everyone else went to bed. The usual bedtime is 8 p.m. but since I was there, they were allowed to stay up until 8:30 p.m.

> Overall social skills like getting along with people are poorly developed and I suspect one reason is that they are not put in frequent contact with people outside the stream of institutional personnel and settings. Because the institution and its life style are still so present in the residents' daily lives, they maintain and regress to institutionalized behavior without testing themselves as to how community life is different from institutional life. Most of the residents have a poor time making decisions or being realistic about their choices.

> G seems to be very lonely in his life in the community. His only relationships are with relatives. He has no peer relationships. He has nothing to occupy his time during the day . . . . G lives with his elderly mother who is too ill to get out of the house. So G is more or less confined there. His mother means well but speaks of him as a "child" or a "kid," not as a 39-year-old man. She will *not* permit him to help around the house, i.e., make his own bed or wash dishes, etc. She says he takes chairs apart and puts them back together again because he has nothing else to do. It appeared to me that G has a lot of potential and it really is a waste of human potential to see him so deprived of meaningful work, friendships, and services. Although he is living at home, it is hardly an atmosphere of normalization.

The comments of the study group members also reflect the problems of restrictive settings. As one person said, *"I don't feel like I'm shut in, but closed in, I feel like. Want to feel more independent, too many rules here.*" Another person stated, "*I hate being restricted when there's no purpose to it. Being restricted from boyfriend, especially by phone or seeing him. When on phone having someone bugging and bothering you. Having people think you can't make your own decisions. People sticking their noses in someone else's business. We also can't wear halter tops.*"

FRIENDSHIPS, ROMANTIC RELATIONSHIPS, AND MARRIAGES

Most study group members (80 percent) had friends when they lived in the institution. At the time they were interviewed, over half of them still visited or kept in touch with these friends. In instances where individuals no longer saw friends from the institution, lack of transportation was the primary reason for losing contact. More moderately and mildly retarded persons maintained contact with friends from the institution than did severely retarded individuals.

At the time of the interviews, 80 percent of the group had good friends. Most frequently, their friends lived in the community, but friends from the institution, staff from community programs, and relatives were also mentioned often as friends. More adults had friends than children (83 and 75 percent, respectively). The frequency of friendships did not differ, however, by level of retardation.

Less than half the group (47 percent) had had romantic relationships since leaving the institution. Such relationships were more common among mildly and moderately retarded persons (62 and 45 percent, respectively) than among severely retarded individuals (24 percent). As we observed earlier, only 60 percent of the study group members were allowed to date and only about one-quarter of the group had gone on dates in the past year. As would be expected, romantic relationships were more common among adults than among children (50 and 31 percent, respectively).

In cases where study group members had been involved in romantic relationships, most of the families (80 percent) indicated that study group members had handled those relationships "all right" or "very well." The remaining 20 percent of the family respondents felt that they had not been managed very well. (See Table VI.4.) Surprisingly, families of mildly retarded people gave lower ratings than families of moderately or severely retarded people. (See Appendix D, Table D.5.)

TABLE VI.4
FAMILY RATINGS OF COMPETENCE IN
MANAGING ROMANTIC RELATIONSHIPS

Managed Relationship	N(201)	%
Very well	100	50
All right	59	29
Not very well	42	21

Similarly, children were rated lower by their families in terms of their handling of romantic relationships than were adults. (See Appendix D, Table D.6.)

Seven study group members were married at the time of the interviews; five of them had children, one person was divorced, and one was separated. The remaining 98 percent of the people had never been married. An interviewer described one of the married study group members in the following way:

> I was rather surprised to find that resident was married and had a family. But I was also very impressed with the way she handled the whole situation. She appears to be a good housekeeper and an excellent mother. Her social worker says she has some difficulty cooking and manging her money, but she tries so hard. She tries with the help of the social worker to learn and understand financial responsibilities. She seems like a warm and generous person who loves both her husband and baby. From what the social worker has told me, her husband isn't the greatest toward her and lives off her SSI check. So, considering everything, I'd say she is adjusting to the real world unbelievably well.

SOCIAL ADJUSTMENT AND RELATIONSHIPS

To find out how study group members were handling their relationships with friends and others (e.g., people at work or school), we asked families if social relationships and loneliness were problems. About one-third of the family respondents indicated that they were. (See Tables VI.5 and VI.6.) When the study group members were questioned in this regard, 21 percent indicated that loneliness was a big problem and 17 percent said that social relationships constituted a big problem for them in the community.

TABLE VI.5
FAMILY PERCEPTIONS OF SOCIAL RELATIONSHIPS
AS A PROBLEM

Extent of Problem	N(437)	%
Big problem	60	14
Somewhat of a problem	105	24
Not a problem	272	62

TABLE VI.6
FAMILY PERCEPTIONS OF LONELINESS AS A PROBLEM

Extent of Problem	N(440)	%
Big problem	48	11
Somewhat of a problem	120	27
Not a problem	272	62

Some of the interviewers' comments help shed light on the kinds of problems experienced by study group members and their families in the social domain. One interviewer summed up her observations as follows:

> Finally, again and again comments were made about the lack of training given to mentally retarded persons about getting along with people. The females all want to get married, have a hard time separating boys as friends and boyfriends — either way, they want marriage out of the relationship. This struck me as being a rather desperate plea for some sort of *real*, deep, profound experience in their lives rather than living on the fringes of activity and experience. Their family lives assume such mammoth importance in the life of a mentally retarded person and they want that same opportunity to create what they have been living with. Given the fact that women in X do marry young and seem to be programmed for it at every turn, it is understandable that marriage for mentally retarded adolescents is seen as a prime goal — yet the supportive services available for that type of relationship are pitifully lacking.

Problems with social relationships and loneliness did not vary according to age but differed greatly according to level of retardation. Fewer families of severely retarded persons than of those who were mildly or moderately retarded indicated that loneliness and social relationships posed problems. (See Appendix D, Tables D.7 and D.8.) For example, about three-quarters of the families of severely retarded persons felt that loneliness and social relationships did *not* pose problems for them, compared to slightly more than half of the families of mildly and moderately retarded study group members.

Again, we must distinguish between actual differences in social adjustment and different expectations of adjustment. Are the severely retarded persons adjusting better than their less retarded peers (according to ratings of family respondents) or do their families and society in general expect less of the severely retarded in terms of social relationships? On the one hand, we found that the severely retarded study group members participated in fewer leisure activities, lived in more restrictive settings, and had fewer friends and romantic relationships than the other people in the study. On the other hand, their families rated their social adjustment in these areas more positively than the families of the less severely retarded individuals. The most plausible explanation for these apparent contradictions is that less is expected of the severely retarded persons in the social realm. Although they have fewer social relationships than other people, their families do not appear to see this as problematic.

Although we asked the study group members themselves about their problems with loneliness and social relationships, it was difficult for them to respond to these questions, particularly in the case of severely retarded persons. Based on the data which we gathered, however, the perceptions of the severely retarded persons were similar to those of the other study group members. On the average, about one-fifth of the group felt that loneliness and social relationships were problems which they encountered in the community.

SUMMARY

As we noted at the beginning of this chapter, data on social activities and relationships are difficult to collect and to interpret. Furthermore, it is hard to determine which standards should be used to assess the quality of mentally retarded people's social experiences. Should we compare their experiences to those of the so-called normal population? We know little about the social lives and relationships of the nonretarded, and we have no comprehensive yardsticks to measure the experiences of retarded and nonretarded individuals. It is therefore difficult to make general statements about the social lives of mentally retarded people living in the community.

One conclusion which can be made, however, is that the social experiences of the study group members were extremely varied. Some individuals functioned well — they were active in a variety of leisure activities and had many friends and satisfying social relationships. Others seemed to exist on the fringes of this domain — if they were active in leisure activities, these were usually solitary rather than social. They had few friends, even fewer romantic relationships, and often lived in residences which did not permit or encourage social independence. Interviewers frequently observed that these individuals needed to be given the opportunity to experience social relationships. Finding leisure activities was a problem for the entire study group, but was particularly troublesome for adults. Adults were least likely to be entertained within the home, and were apparently not able to find appropriate spare-time activities outside the home.

Although most of the study group members were reported to have friends, many individuals apparently had none in the community, and loneliness was mentioned as one of the biggest problems faced by all study group members. Thus, as we observed earlier, the opportunities for social experiences and for establishing social relationships appear to be inadequate for many retarded people living in the community.

Chapter VII

What Are They Getting: Services

A major component in successful deinstitutionalization is the development of a flexible network of community support systems which are responsive to the changing needs of retarded persons and their families. Recognizing the importance of such supports, we explored the extent to which mentally retarded persons and their families need and use various types of services. The crucial need for support of all kinds was echoed by both retarded persons and their families. For example, when asked what worried him, one mentally retarded person responded, *"Having no one to help me if something happens. I'm afraid of strange, new places, of getting lost or having no one to help me."* Another replied, *"Everything [worries me]. About what you're gonna do in the community and how you're going to get along with people. Like food and money and how to handle it."*

Parents and families as well as the mentally retarded individuals themselves, are concerned that appropriate care and support are available as retarded people — both young and old — move from the institution to the community. One parent expressed this concern succinctly: *"I'm worried about the future. These changes are encouraging the retarded to be more independent. Sometimes it's as hard on me as on her [the retarded daughter]. It's hard for me to learn her true limits just like it's hard on her. But now I'm here. What happens when I'm not?"*

We asked a series of questions concerning the types of personal support and institutional follow-up (i.e., contact by staff from the releasing institution) provided in the community. We also obtained information on the types of services provided to retarded persons and to the families caring for them.

SOURCES OF PERSONAL SUPPORT

One of the most important kinds of support in the community is the presence of another person who can be contacted for guidance or help. For mentally retarded persons, there are three sources for personal support: staff from the releasing institution, community-based case managers, and nonprofessional individuals, such as relatives or friends.

Less than two-thirds of the retarded persons (60 percent) received any institutional follow-up after their release. (See Table VII.1.) The number receiving follow-up was slightly greater during the first six months after release than during the six months just prior to the interviews. It is difficult to assess this finding conclusively, although several interpretations may be suggested. Some institutions have been criticized for "dumping" their residents into the community with no or little continued responsibility for their welfare. Other institutions have been charged with maintaining excessively strong ties with released individuals. Different institutions claim different degrees of responsibility for released people, as do communities. In regard to the study group, it is possible that institutions only provided follow-up if it was considered necessary in a particular case, rather than as a general policy. (As we mentioned in Chapter III, less than 70 percent of the study group members were released from institutions which indicated that they had a continued responsibility for released individuals.) Some institutions may not have had the staff resources to provide follow-up, or it may have been provided by the community social worker with family respondents unaware that follow-up had occurred. For whatever reasons follow-up did or did not occur, many families felt that the individual had been released without adequate follow-up from the institution and without provision of adequate services in the community.

TABLE VII.1
SOURCES OF PERSONAL SUPPORT OR FOLLOW-UP

Source	Has Received or Receives		Has Not Received/ Does Not Receive		Total	
	N	%	N	%	N	%
Institutional follow-up	264	60	176	40	440	100
Community case manager	427	97	13	3	440	100
Nonprofessional individual (relative or friend)	324	74	116	26	440	100

For those released persons who did receive follow-up, it generally occurred on a monthly basis. The most common form of follow-up was a visit to the person's home by an institutional staff member, or contact through a third person (i.e., the institutional staff member contacted the community social worker or someone else in touch with the released person).

Almost all family respondents (97 percent) said that there was a "case manager" in the community for the retarded person — someone responsible for securing appropriate services. About one-third indicated that a social worker or someone from a community agency served as case manager. However, about 40 percent of the respondents said that a parent (natural, foster, or house manager) acted as case manager, indicating that for many retarded persons, there is no formal professional or state-sponsored case manager *outside the home* who is responsible for ensuring that adequate care is provided. This is an important consideration, particularly for natural parents who are concerned about locating services and who fear that no one will be responsible for securing adequate care should they no longer be able to assume this responsibility.

In addition to a case manager who is formally charged with providing or securing needed services, it is also important that retarded persons have someone they can turn to for personal support and guidance on an informal basis. While almost three-quarters of the study group (74 percent) reportedly had access to such a person, it is perhaps more significant that nearly one-quarter did not. In particular, we found that over one-third of the severely retarded and nearly half the children had no one in the community to whom they could turn for personal support. (See Appendix E, Tables E.1 and E.2.) For those who did have someone to turn to, relatives, teachers, and community friends were most often cited as providing this kind of personal support. However, severely retarded persons differed from the rest of the group in that very few were said to have friends or peers who filled this need.

COMMUNITY SUPPORT SERVICES

Four types of services for the retarded person were selected for inclusion in this study, each relating to a fundamental aspect of community existence:

- medical and health care (including medical, dental, speech therapy, and physical therapy services);

- social and recreational (including recreational and occupational therapy, social services, and camp programs);

- employment and job training; and

- housing and legal services.

In addition, many communities offer support services to the families (parents, guardians, or group home managers) of mentally retarded persons. We investigated the following services for families:

- support and/or training prior to the mentally retarded person's release;

- general counseling;

- consultation with professionals concerning specific problems, needs, or changes in the mentally retarded person's life;

- temporary relief from responsibilities; and

- professional or parent associations to maintain contact and share information with other professionals or parents.

For each type of service we asked four questions:

- Has this service been used since the person's release to the community?

- If not, is the service needed?

- Who provides the service?

- How frequently is this service used?

The responses to these questions provided a great deal of valuable information on the support services used or received by mentally retarded persons and their families (see Tables VII.2 and VII.6) on the range of sources for such services (see Tables VII.3 and VII.7) and on the frequency with which such services were provided (Tables VII.4 and VII.8).*

---

*It is important to note that we made no attempt to verify the accuracy of the responses. For example, some respondents may have said a service was not received when, in fact, the retarded person did receive it through a third party. Similarly, some respondents may have reported that a service was received monthly, when, in fact, the mentally retarded person received the service weekly. However, the *perception* of a service being available or received may bear strongly on the assumed range of options and expectations of those responsible for ensuring appropriate care for retarded persons.

TABLE VII.2
UTILIZATION OF AND NEED FOR SUPPORT SERVICES

Type of Service	Received		Needed, Not Received		Not Needed, Not Received		Total	
	N	%	N	%	N	%	N	%
Medical and Health Care								
Medical care	410	93	4	1	26	6	440	100
Dental services	333	76	37	8	69	16	439	100
Physical therapy	46	11	25	6	367	83	438	100
Speech therapy	124	28	72	17	242	55	438	100
Social and Recreational Services								
Recreational therapy	354	80	39	9	47	11	440	100
Social and psychological therapy	247	57	37	8	153	35	437	100
Camp programs	165	43	52	13	171	44	388	100
Occupational therapy	140	32	40	9	260	59	440	100
Employment Services								
Employment placement and support services	218	50	25	6	193	44	436	100
Housing and Legal Services								
Housing assistance	102	23	8	2	330	75	440	100
Legal assistance	41	9	9	2	390	89	440	100
Average		46		7		47		

TABLE VII.3
SOURCES OF SUPPORT SERVICES

Type of Service	Institution		Residence		Day/Work Program		Community Agency		Private Services		Total	
	N	%	N	%	N	%	N	%	N	%	N	%
Medical and Health Care												
Medical care	93	19	36	7	8	2	189	38	168	34	494	100
Dental services	95	25	20	5	5	1	130	33	140	36	390	100
Physical therapy	14	17	12	15	18	23	33	42	2	3	79	100
Speech therapy	17	9	24	13	61	34	74	41	6	3	182	100
Social and Recreational Services												
Recreational therapy	22	4	212	37	130	23	207	36	1	>1	572	100
Social and psychological therapy	51	15	56	16	55	16	164	49	12	4	338	100
Camp programs	17	8	26	13	27	13	131	65	1	1	202	100
Occupational therapy	6	4	31	19	88	55	33	21	2	1	160	100
Employment Services												
Employment placement and support services	34	12	44	16	116	41	84	30	3	1	281	100
Housing and Legal Services												
Housing assistance	7	6	38	34	4	3	63	56	1	1	113	100
Legal assistance	3	6	14	27	6	12	21	40	8	15	52	100
Total	359	13	513	18	518	18	1129	39	344	12	2863	100

a The totals represent the total number of sources from which services were received. A single type of service may have been provided by multiple sources.

TABLE VII.4
FREQUENCY OF SERVICE UTILIZATION

Type of Service	Not Received		Received at Least Once/Week		Received at Least Once/Month		Received at Least Once/Year		Total	
	N	%	N	%	N	%	N	%	N	%
Medical and Health Care										
Medical care	30	7	12	3	71	16	321	74	434	100
Dental services	106	24	1	>1	17	4	314	72	438	100
Physical therapy	392	90	31	7	5	1	8	2	436	100
Speech therapy	314	72	104	24	10	2	10	2	438	100
Social and Recreational Services										
Recreational therapy	86	20	278	64	56	13	14	3	434	100
Social and psychological therapy	190	43	61	14	96	22	92	21	439	100
Camp programs	223	57	7	2	2	1	156	40	388	100
Occupational therapy	300	70	96	22	22	5	14	3	432	100
Employment Services										
Employment placement and support services	218	50	90	20	60	14	68	16	436	100
Housing and Legal Services										
Housing assistance	332	77	16	4	5	1	79	18	432	100
Legal assistance	399	91	1	>1	6	1	34	8	440	100

Medical and Health Care

The service used most widely by mentally retarded persons was medical care. Nearly all (93 percent) had received some medical treatment since release, generally once a year. The most common providers were community agencies and private physicians. Very few individuals (less than 1 percent) were said to be in need of medical care but not receiving it. Not surprisingly, 91 percent of the family respondents said that meeting the retarded persons' medical needs was not a problem. (See Table VII.5.) Nearly all the mentally retarded persons gave the same response.

TABLE VII.5
PROBLEMS ENCOUNTERED BY FAMILIES
IN OBTAINING SERVICES

Type of Problem	Has Been/Is a Problem		Has Not Been/Is Not a Problem		Total	
	N	%	N	%	N	%
Meeting retarded person's medical needs	35	9	349	91	384	100
Meeting retarded person's psychological needs	83	22	300	78	383	100
Lack of support services for mentally retarded person in the community	104	27	277	73	381	100
Lack of support services for family in the community	72	19	310	81	382	100

Dental services were obtained by about three-quarters of the study group members on a yearly basis. Again, community agencies and private clinics were the most common providers. However, children were more often treated by the institution from which they were released than were adult retarded persons. (See Appendix E, Table E.4.) Almost one-fifth of the children were not receiving dental attention and were said to need it. (See Appendix E, Table E.3.)

Speech therapy was the service most frequently reported to be needed but not received. Almost one-fifth of the study group members were described as being in need of speech therapy. The need was even greater among children (24 percent) and among severely retarded individuals (30 percent). (See Appendix E, Tables E.3 and E.5, respectively.)

Since speech impediments were the most common additional disability among the study group members, it is not surprising that many needed speech therapy. What is surprising is the apparent absence of community services to meet the need. Speech therapy was used by a little more than one-quarter of the total group (28 percent), the service being provided primarily through community agencies and day programs on a weekly basis.

Unlike speech therapy, physical therapy was one of the least used or needed services, with only 11 percent of the group receiving it. In general, physical therapy was received on a weekly basis from community agencies. The small need for physical therapy is not surprising when it is recalled that only about 15 percent of the study group had some mobility impairment (predominantly children and the severely retarded). Although only 6 percent of the group needed the service but did not receive it, children were twice as likely as adults and severely retarded were at least three times as likely as mildly and moderately retarded individuals to need physical therapy but not receive it.

In summary, medical and health care needs were generally well provided in the community with the sole exception of speech therapy. Medical and dental services were received by the majority of released persons. Physical and speech therapy services were received by considerably fewer. In general, a higher proportion of children than adults were described as having unmet medical needs, particularly for dental care and speech therapy.

Social and Recreational Services

As discussed in Chapter VI, social and recreational activities play a central role in the lives of persons living in the community. The study group members frequently mentioned their desire to meet new people and become less isolated. However, not all communities provide the level or breadth of social and recreational services required to meet these needs.

Social and psychological counseling was received by slightly more than half the total group, and was provided primarily by community agencies. Adults and mildly retarded persons tended to use such services most often. Since psychological problems were somewhat more prevalent among mildly retarded persons, it is not surprising that they tended to have the greatest unmet need for such services.

Interviewers frequently noted that the absence of adequate psychological support services for individuals with behavior difficulties was a major problem for their families. Indeed, almost one-quarter of the families felt that meeting the psychological needs of the mentally retarded person in their care was a substantial problem. (See Table VII.5.) One interviewer provided the following example,

> She [the mother, Mrs. S.] says he [W] is very uncooperative about most things they request of him . . . . He curses at them, especially his mother, and sometimes hits her. He broke his brother's nose. Mrs. S. feels that he can be dangerous. Mrs. S.'s most frequent complaint is that she is unaware of any source of help or relief for W. Although one of the social workers at the institution seems to have taken an interest in the S's, she has not offered any alternatives to them. They stressed the fact that they do not know of any community services to help them and they just do not know what to do with W at this point. Mr. and Mrs. S. seemed to care very much about W's best interests, but they feel totally overwhelmed by his behavioral maladjustment to them and the community.

Recreational services seemed to be more prevalent, although as we discussed in Chapter V, unmet needs in this area also presented somewhat of a problem for many families. About 80 percent of the total group used some type of recreational service in the community (64 percent used it on a weekly basis). The residence was the most common source of this service. Less than half the group attended camp once a year. About one-third of the group received some type of occupational therapy, generally as part of their day programs. In general, utilization was somewhat more common among severely retarded than among mildly or moderately retarded individuals, and unmet need was slightly greater among mildly retarded individuals.

Employment Services

The employability of mentally retarded persons is one of the most critical factors in their ability to support themselves as well as be supported in the community. Thus, finding and maintaining a job are among the major concerns of mentally retarded persons and their families. Almost half of the study group members had received some form of job counseling or training since their release. It was generally provided as part of the day activity or school program in which the individual participated or at his or her place of employment. About 6 percent of the study group members were reported to be in need of employment services but not receiving them. Less than one-third of the severely retarded persons had received employment placement and support services, and not surprisingly, only 16 percent of the children had received them. (See Chapter V for further discussion of work needs and opportunities.)

Housing and Legal Services

Housing and legal assistance tend to be used on a short-term or one-shot basis. Most of the study group members neither used nor needed either kind of service. About one-quarter of the group had received housing assistance, and about 10 percent had used legal services. Many more adults and mildly retarded individuals received housing assistance than did children and more retarded people. This may be related to the fact that older, less retarded people are more likely to be living independently, thus requiring some type of assistance in finding housing. In general, there was little unmet need for these services.

It is worth noting that a relatively small number of individuals needed legal assistance. This is probably related to the fact that fewer than 10 percent of the study group members had difficulty staying out of trouble with the law. (See the discussion in Chapter IX.)

COMMUNITY SERVICES FOR FAMILIES OF RETARDED PERSONS

The utilization of support services by families can be a crucial factor in improving and maintaining their ability to deal with the mentally retarded member of the household. We identified five types of services offered to families.

The first service which is likely to be provided is training *prior to* the retarded person's placement in the home to prepare the parents for the individual's arrival. About one-third of the families indicated that they had received such training, and another quarter felt that they needed but did not receive it. (See Table VII.6.) Indeed, it was the service which was most frequently needed but not received by families. It is important to note that although three-quarters of the families received training from some community source, only 28 percent received training from the institution. (See Table VII.7.) This is particularly interesting because half the study group members were released from institutions which indicated that it was their policy to provide some type of training to families prior to the individual's release. Thus, although institutions are an important source of this crucial service, they apparently are not providing it as frequently as their policies would indicate.

TABLE VII.6
UTILIZATION OF AND NEED FOR SUPPORT SERVICES FOR FAMILIES OF RETARDED PERSONS

Type of Service	Received		Needed, Not Received		Not Needed, Not Received		Total	
	N	%	N	%	N	%	N	%
Support and/or training prior to individual's release	125	32	103	26	168	42	296	100
General counseling	216	55	47	12	132	33	395	100
Consultation for handling specific problems	305	77	29	7	65	16	399	100
Temporary relief from responsibilities	217	61	36	10	104	29	357	100
Parent or professional associations	166	42	65	16	165	42	396	100
Average		53		14		32		

TABLE VII.7
SOURCES OF SUPPORT SERVICES FOR FAMILIES OF RETARDED PERSONS

Type of Service	Institution		Residence		Day/Work Program		Community Agency		Private Provider		Total	
	N(284)	%	N(205)	%	N(60)	%	N(650)	%	N(33)	%	N	%
Support and/or training prior to individual's release	45	28	28	17	3	2	77	47	10	6	163	100
General counseling	70	27	26	10	15	6	139	55	5	2	255	100
Consultation for handling specific problems	104	27	49	13	27	7	187	49	14	4	381	100
Temporary relief from responsibilities	59	26	95	41	9	4	65	28	1	1	229	100
Parent or professional associations	6	3	7	4	6	3	182	89	3	1	204	100
Total	284	23	205	17	60	5	650	52	33	3	1232	100

In addition to training and counseling available prior to the individual's release, two types of services may be available to families following the individual's release: consultation for help in handling specific problems, and general counseling. The single service most commonly used by families was consultation in regard to specific problems. Over three-quarters of the families used this service, generally on a regular basis. Indeed, consultation was the only service used by over half the families at least once a month (including 28 percent who were receiving it at least once a week — see Table VII.8). Also, consultation for handling specific problems was the service which fewest families needed but did not receive (7 percent).

General counseling, on the other hand, was used by slightly more than half the families, and less than one-third of the families were receiving it at least once a month (including those who used it at least once a week). About 12 percent of the families indicated they needed but did not receive general counseling services.

About 60 percent of the families had respite care or temporary relief from their responsibilities, which was generally available on a weekly basis. For many, this was one of the most important support services connected with their work. Most reported that "time out" was very difficult to obtain and that they were virtually on call around the clock. One house manager said her biggest problem was that she did not have any time to be by herself, or to go out for a free evening with friends, and that the community agency responsible for the home simply did not have the resources to remedy the problem. This was not an uncommon predicament; many interviewers noted the sense of isolation and lack of personal freedom among families and staff caring for mentally retarded individuals. Surprisingly, only 10 percent of the families indicated that they needed relief but were not receiving it.

There were some differences according to the individual's age and level of retardation. In general, families of children used somewhat fewer services and had more unmet needs than did families of adults. (See Appendix E, Table E.6.) Similarly, families caring for severely retarded persons utilized fewer services and had more unmet needs than did families of less retarded persons. (See Appendix E, Table E.7.)

Differences among various types of residences were even more marked. (See Table VII.9.) Natural families had by far the lowest utilization rate on almost all the services: only about one-fifth of all natural families used each type of service. It may be recalled that children were more likely to be placed in their natural homes than were adults. Thus, it appears that many natural families with mentally retarded children are receiving far fewer services than other types of

TABLE VII.8
FREQUENCY OF SERVICE UTILIZATION FOR FAMILIES OF RETARDED PERSONS

Type of Service	Not Received		Received at Least Once/Week		Received at Least Once/Month		Received at Least Once/Year		Total	
	N	%	N	%	N	%	N	%	N	%
Support and/or training prior to individual's release	271	70	50	13	20	5	48	12	389	100
General counseling	181	46	57	15	64	16	92	23	394	100
Consultation for handling specific problems	92	23	110	28	116	30	74	19	392	100
Temporary relief from responsibilities	140	39	103	29	34	10	79	22	356	100
Parent or professional associations	230	60	25	6	80	21	52	13	387	100

TABLE VII.9
UTILIZATION OF AND NEED FOR SUPPORT SERVICES
FOR FAMILIES OF RETARDED PERSONS BY TYPE OF RESIDENCE

Type of Service	Setting	Received		Needed, Not Received		Not Needed, Not Received		Total	
		N	%	N	%	N	%	N	%
Support and/or training prior to individual's release	Natural home	4	8	15	30	31	62	50	100
	Foster home	18	33	8	14	29	53	55	100
	Group home	63	34	62	34	59	32	184	100
	Semi-independent home	20	43	4	8	23	49	47	100
General counseling	Natural home	7	15	10	21	31	64	48	100
	Foster home	8	17	8	17	30	66	46	100
	Group home	149	70	21	10	43	20	213	100
	Semi-independent home	29	66	4	9	11	25	44	100
Consultation for handling specific problems	Natural home	18	34	10	19	25	47	53	100
	Foster home	30	60	6	12	14	28	50	100
	Group home	175	88	7	3	18	9	200	100
	Semi-independent home	38	91	1	2	3	7	42	100
Temporary relief from responsibilities	Natural home	13	26	12	24	25	50	50	100
	Foster home	24	45	1	2	28	53	53	100
	Group home	148	76	15	8	31	16	194	100
	Semi-independent home	2	13	2	13	11	74	15	100
Parent or professional associations	Natural home	14	28	11	22	25	50	50	100
	Foster home	22	42	2	4	29	54	53	100
	Group home	90	48	38	21	58	31	186	100
	Semi-independent home	18	45	5	13	17	42	40	100
Average	Natural home		22		23		55		
	Foster ho.ne		39		10		51		
	Group home		63		15		22		
	Semi-independent home		52		9		39		

residential placements. For example, only 8 percent of the natural families had received any type of training or support prior to the return of their child, whereas one-third to almost one-half of the other kinds of families had received such assistance.

Group home and semi-independent living staff received the most assistance (63 and 52 percent, respectively), which may reflect a higher degree of professionalism among these families. Staff in virtually all these settings received consultation on specific problems and the majority also received ongoing general counseling. Temporary relief services were used in over three-quarters of the group homes. About twice as many foster families as natural families used all services, with an average utilization rate of 39 percent.

An average of nearly one-quarter of the natural families expressed an unmet need for each support service. While group homes tended to utilize the most services, many also expressed an unmet need for services. This may reflect a greater awareness on the part of group home staff of the types of services available. Further, group homes have traditionally been more willing than other residences to care for severely retarded persons; because of this fact they may have a greater need for outside help and consultation. Staff in semi-independent homes were least likely to express unmet needs for services, perhaps because of the greater independence of residents in these settings. Also, staff in semi-independent homes generally have more free time for themselves.

SUMMARY

The process of deinstitutionalization requires both the retarded person's adjustment to the community and the adaptation of the community to the needs of *all* its citizens. The services available in the community to support both the retarded person and his or her family are an extremely important part of this process. According to our interview data, study group members were receiving a broad array of services and relatively few families felt that services were needed but not received.

Overall, an average of 46 percent of the mentally retarded people were reported to have used each of the 11 services, and an average of only 7 percent needed services which were not received. Nevertheless, over one-quarter of the families felt that obtaining adequate support services for the retarded person posed at least somewhat of a problem for them. Perhaps this indicates that even when services were used they may not have been adequate or may have required considerable effort to obtain. As might be expected, medical and health care services were more frequently received than other types of services. The sole exception was speech therapy, for which there was the greatest expression of unmet need (17 percent).

Use of support services for families was more common than use of services for the mentally retarded individuals, with about half of the families, on the average, using each type of support service. Families also expressed more unmet needs for their own support services than for services for the retarded person. However, only about one-fifth of the families felt that obtaining support for themselves was a problem, compared to one-quarter who felt that obtaining services for the mentally retarded person was a problem. In general, natural families both received fewer services and had a greater unmet need for support than other types of families. In this respect, the service most lacking was support and training prior to the arrival of the mentally retarded person in the home.

On the average, the most common providers of support services to retarded people and their families were community agencies, which provided an average of 39 percent of the services received by the study group members and 52 percent of those received by the families. Interestingly, institutions were a more common source of service for families than for retarded individuals: 23 and 12 percent, respectively. For both groups, the residence itself provided less than one-fifth of the services. Nor surprisingly, retarded people received considerably more services through their day programs than did the families. In fact, almost 90 percent of the services received by the mentally retarded people were provided by noninstitutional community sources. However, it is also important to remember that the parent (natural or foster parent, or house manager) served as case manager for 40 percent of the study group. The vital role of the parents or families in securing services for mentally retarded persons may indicate the absence of a well developed community support system through which the community assumes responsibility for its retarded citizens.

Perhaps one of the most significant findings was that nearly one-quarter of the mentally retarded persons had no special person outside the home to turn to in a personal crisis or simply for friendship. This may be the one "service" which a community cannot provide but which marks the difference between the retarded person's isolated, lonely existence in the community and a life which derives meaning from the sense of belonging and being cared *about* rather than solely being care *for.*

Chapter VIII
What Are They Getting: Training

I think people should be taught things to provide your own needs, better cooking, shopping, education in the community, better relationships with neighbors and people on the job and all.
(statement by a retarded woman)

The range and types of skills that the retarded individual needs to live in the community are essentially the same as those which the non-retarded person requires. The differences lie in the generally more prolonged training needs of retarded persons, and the use of different training strategies and techniques. Persons who may have successfully adjusted to institutional life but who are now confronted with a much richer and more demanding life in the community must learn numerous new skills. Also many previously acquired skills may be in need of reinforcement as the new ones are learned. Both the similarities and the differences in the training needs of retarded and non-retarded people are apparent in one woman's response when asked what she had recently learned to do: *"Wash my own clothes, which I didn't get to learn in the institution. I learned right away when I moved to town. I learned a little cooking. Liver, I learned to make. I've got to make that sometime as soon as I get a frying pan. Defrost the refrigerator — I haven't done that yet."*

We investigated six major categories of training encompassing 24 kinds of skills which mentally retarded individuals must acquire in order to live in the community. Note that these are the same categories which we used to investigate the kinds and extent of training provided in the institution (see Chapter III).

- personal maintenance: eating, using the toilet, dressing and undressing, cleanliness and grooming skills;
- sensory development: motor coordination and development, sensory proficiency in hearing and vision, and speech and language development;

- education and employment: preacademic (such as shapes, colors, and sizes), recognition of numbers and telling time, reading and writing, prevocational (such as punctuality and cooperation), vocational (specific job) skills;

- domestic living: housekeeping, meal preparation, shopping, money management skills;

- use of community resources: travel and mobility, use of the telephone, dealing with emergencies, learning to use community agencies;

- behavior management: interpersonal relations, behavior control, recreational and social behavior development.

For each of the 24 kinds of skills, we asked the following questions to yield information both on the training which was received and that which was not received:

Has the individual received this training since release?
(If yes:)

Who provides the training?

How frequently is the training provided?

(If no, why does he or she not need this training?)

Because he or she already has the skill?

Because he or she is not yet ready for the skill?

Responses to these questions provide an indication of the types of training currently available to retarded persons in the community — reflecting one aspect of the community's readiness to support mentally retarded persons. Furthermore, families' responses permit some insight into the family perceptions of the individual's readiness to acquire new skills. A statement that the person is not yet ready for training may represent an accurate assessment of the individual's current capabilities, or it may reflect the family's inappropriately low expectations of the persons capabilities. It is, of course, impossible to assess the accuracy of such information. However, regardless of whether or not a particular judgment is accurate, the family's assessment is likely to have a strong bearing on the range of training considered important for the mentally retarded person.

In many instances, family respondents knew what kinds of training had been received. In other cases, they surmised that training in a particular skill had been provided because the person was proficient in that skill. However, that proficiency may have been the result of earlier institutional training. Thus, the data may overstate the amount of community-based training received. On the other hand, many family respondents noted that even when training had been provided, it may not have been adequate to meet the individual's need.

There was considerable variation in the amount of training received in the six major skill areas by the study group members. The greatest amount of training was in the behavior management category, with about three-quarters of the study group receiving training in each of the three skills in this category. (See Table VIII.1.) Training in sensory development was least commonly received — having been provided to about one-third of the study group. However, very few persons who had not received sensory development training were reported to need it.

About two-thirds of the study group members received training in domestic living skills. Over half the individuals received training in education and employment skills, and almost half were trained in personal maintenance skills. Finally, a little more than one-third of the people were trained to use community resources.

There were only three types of skills for which less than one-quarter of the study group received training: hearing and vision proficiency, using the toilet, and using community agencies. Very few individuals were reported to need training in these skills. Most had already acquired the first two kinds of skills, and many were not considered by their families to be ready to receive training in the third.

There were only three specific skill areas in which 10 percent or more of the study group members did not receive training and were thought to be in need of it: speech and language development (10 percent), coping with emergencies (11 percent), and using community agencies (10 percent). The latter two types of training represent more advanced aspects of living in the community for which very little training was provided in the institution (see Chapter III). More than half the family respondents felt that the individual was not yet ready to be trained in using community agencies, and almost one-third made the same judgment in regard to coping with emergencies.

Thus, study group members generally either had received or were receiving training in basic skill areas (such as personal maintenance and domestic skills) and in behavior management. Training in some of the more complex community skills, such as money management,

TABLE VIII.1
UTILIZATION OF AND NEED FOR TRAINING

Type of Training	Received		Needed, Not Received		Not Needed, Not Received				Total	
					Already Had Skill		Not Ready For Skill			
	N	%	N	%	N	%	N	%	N	%
Personal Maintenance										
Eating	211	57	4	1	153	41	2	1	370	100
Using the toilet	67	19	3	1	284	79	7	1	361	100
Dressing	103	28	4	1	255	70	5	1	367	100
Cleanliness	242	64	3	1	127	34	5	1	377	100
Grooming	246	65	3	1	119	31	10	3	378	100
Sensory Development										
Motor	131	31	19	4	274	64	5	1	429	100
Hearing and vision	77	18	9	2	336	79	2	1	424	100
Speech and language	218	50	42	10	156	36	19	4	435	100
Education and Employment										
Preacademic	118	34	12	3	207	60	9	3	346	100
Numbers and telling time	249	59	32	8	96	23	44	10	421	100
Reading and writing	253	59	40	9	64	15	71	17	428	100
Prevocational	276	64	16	4	77	18	62	14	431	100
Vocational	218	51	34	8	44	10	133	31	429	100
Domestic Living										
Housekeeping	293	69	11	3	105	24	17	4	426	100
Meal preparation	320	73	17	4	60	14	43	9	440	100
Shopping	271	62	18	4	69	16	81	18	439	100
Money management	270	61	34	8	38	9	98	22	440	100
Use of Community Resources										
Travel and mobility	219	49	30	7	106	25	84	19	439	100
Using the telephone	176	41	28	7	126	29	99	23	429	100
Coping with emergencies	192	44	50	11	72	16	124	29	438	100
Using community agencies	96	22	42	10	56	13	238	55	432	100
Behavior Management										
Interpersonal relationships	342	78	20	5	61	14	16	3	439	100
Behavior control	317	72	12	3	98	22	11	3	438	100
Social and recreational activities	350	80	18	4	61	14	10	2	439	100

using the telephone, and shopping, was less common. Not surprisingly, these patterns varied according to age and level of retardation. (See Appendix F, Tables F.1 and F.2.) Children and severely retarded persons were less likely to have received training in many areas and were more likely to not be ready to receive training, as compared with adults and mildly retarded persons.

The source of training varied considerably for the different types of skills. (See Table VIII.2.) According to family respondents, community residences provided over three-quarters of the study group members with training in personal maintenance and domestic living skills, and also provided over half of them with training in community use and behavior management skills. In many cases, day or work programs were the source of training in sensory development, education and employment, and community use skills.

Institutions were cited only infrequently as sources of training for released mentally retarded persons — generally, in sensory development skills, which they provided to less than 10 percent of all study group members. It may be recalled that institutions provided a considerable amount of family support services (about 22 percent) and some of the support services for the mentally retarded individual (about 11 percent). Thus, it appears that the institution is used much less as a source for training than for support services.

Almost all training was provided on at least a weekly basis. (See Table VIII.3.) The only areas in which 10 percent or more of the study group members received training on a monthly basis were coping with emergencies (17 percent), shopping (12 percent), and social and recreational activities (11 percent).

Beyond these overall trends, there were notable variations within each of the six major categories of training. The rest of this chapter is devoted to a discussion of the findings which substantially differed from the overall picture of the types and sources of community-based training for mentally retarded persons.

PERSONAL MAINTENANCE SKILLS

As previously noted, personal maintenance skills were well developed among study group members; virtually no one needed the training who was not receiving it. Well over half the persons received training in eating, cleanliness, and grooming skills. About one-third of the group did not need additional training in these areas. Only about one-quarter of the group received training in using the toilet and dressing and undressing.

TABLE VIII.2
SOURCES OF TRAINING

Type of Training	Institution		Residence		Day/Work Program		Community Agency		Total	
	N	%	N	%	N	%	N	%	N	%
Personal Maintenance										
Eating	1	1	202	73	55	20	18	6	276	100
Using the toilet	1	2	70	69	26	25	5	4	102	100
Dressing	—	—	102	77	22	17	8	6	132	100
Cleanliness	1	1	230	75	56	18	21	6	308	100
Grooming	2	1	235	73	61	19	25	7	323	100
Sensory Development										
Motor	11	6	77	43	75	42	17	9	180	100
Hearing and vision	9	8	37	34	42	38	22	20	110	100
Speech and language	19	6	132	40	121	36	60	18	332	100
Education and Employment										
Preacademic	15	6	76	29	131	50	39	15	261	100
Numbers and telling time	12	3	142	39	154	43	52	15	360	100
Reading and writing	6	2	132	37	162	45	58	16	358	100
Prevocational	8	2	112	29	209	55	54	14	383	100
Vocational	5	2	25	10	183	72	41	16	254	100
Domestic Living										
Housekeeping	2	1	264	76	56	16	26	7	348	100
Meal preparation	1	1	303	75	70	17	28	7	402	100
Shopping	4	1	239	70	62	18	39	11	344	100
Money management	8	2	209	53	126	32	52	13	395	100
Use of Community Resources										
Travel and mobility	3	1	196	64	66	22	41	13	306	100
Using the telephone	3	1	162	69	51	22	20	8	236	100
Coping with emergencies	3	1	175	66	54	20	33	13	265	100
Using community agencies	1	1	80	60	18	13	35	26	134	100
Behavior Management										
Interpersonal relationships	12	2	287	51	178	32	85	15	562	100
Behavior control	13	3	279	54	163	32	60	11	515	100
Social and recreational activities	16	2	271	47	176	31	114	20	577	100

TABLE VIII.3
FREQUENCY OF TRAINING

Type of Training	Not Received		Received at Least Once/Week		Received at Least Once/Month		Received at Least Once/Year		Total	
	N	%	N	%	N	%	N	%	N	%
Personal Maintenance										
Eating	170	44	202	53	2	1	6	2	380	100
Using the toilet	312	82	62	16	2	1	4	1	380	100
Dressing	279	73	97	25	2	1	2	1	380	100
Cleanliness	141	37	228	60	7	2	4	1	380	100
Grooming	139	36	234	61	6	2	2	1	381	100
Sensory Development										
Motor	317	72	108	25	10	2	3	1	438	100
Hearing and vision	368	84	51	12	2	1	19	3	440	100
Speech and language	219	50	201	46	8	2	8	2	436	100
Education and Employment										
Preacademic	249	57	178	41	6	1	1	1	434	100
Numbers and telling time	187	43	237	55	6	2	—	—	430	100
Reading and writing	184	43	241	56	7	1	—	—	432	100
Prevocational	161	37	259	60	6	1	7	2	433	100
Vocational	218	50	194	45	16	3	7	2	435	100
Domestic Living										
Housekeeping	145	33	279	64	7	2	2	1	433	100
Meal preparation	128	29	291	66	16	4	4	1	439	100
Shopping	177	40	206	47	53	12	4	1	440	100
Money management	179	41	226	52	29	6	4	1	438	100
Use of Community Resources										
Travel and mobility	220	51	159	36	39	9	18	4	436	100
Use of the telephone	268	61	129	29	34	8	9	2	440	100
Coping with emergencies	250	57	88	20	73	17	27	6	438	100
Using community agencies	334	78	36	8	37	9	22	5	429	100
Behavior Management										
Interpersonal relationships	107	24	295	67	31	7	7	2	440	100
Behavior control	132	30	262	60	33	8	11	2	438	100
Social and recreational activities	98	26	229	61	43	11	5	2	375	100

Not surprisingly, adults were more proficient than children in the personal maintenance skills. (See Appendix F, Table F.1.) At least half the children were receiving this training; most of those who were not receiving it were said to have already mastered the skills. Very few were not considered ready to learn the skills.

Again as expected, mildly and moderately retarded persons were considerably more skilled in personal maintenance than were severely retarded people. (See Appendix F, Table F.2.) While most severely retarded persons were receiving such training if they were thought to need it, some were not receiving the training because they were not considered ready for it.

SENSORY DEVELOPMENT SKILLS

Of the types of training included in this category (motor, hearing and vision, and speech), speech training was received most commonly. Half of the study group received speech training while 10 percent needed it but did not receive it. In all areas of sensory development, more children than adults and more severely retarded than mildly or moderately retarded individuals received training. About three-quarters of the severely retarded persons received speech and language development training.

We noted in Chapters III and VII that speech impediments were a common problem for which inadequate services existed. This is illustrated by comments made by both mentally retarded persons and interviewers. For example, one study group member said she wanted *"to be better at the long vowel sounds and the short vowel sounds."* Another told an interviewer, *"I have a speech problem and people react and laugh and get upset. I don't like to be around those people."*

Several interviewers commented on the extreme care with which mentally retarded respondents answered questions. For example.

> Mr. T. is verbal and pauses before he says anything as he mentally constructs a full sentence. Given patience, he can respond to any question articulately and succinctly. I was impressed by the obvious effort he made to give me complete answers.

EDUCATION AND EMPLOYMENT*

Over half the study group received training in numbers and telling time, reading and writing, and prevocational and vocational skills.

---

* Education and employment opportunities are discussed at greater length in Chapter V.

About one-third received training in preacademic skills, and there was virtually no one who needed such training but did not receive it. Unmet need was most critical in reading and writing skills and in vocational training.

Nearly three-quarters of the children in the study group received training in educational skills, while less than half received employment training. One-quarter of the children were not considered by their families to be ready to receive training in reading and writing; over half were not judged to be ready for vocational training.

In many cases, similar assessments were made in regard to vocational training for severely retarded individuals. Over one-third were not receiving training in reading and writing, over one-quarter were not receiving training in prevocational skills, and over one-half were not receiving vocational training because they were not yet ready for these skills, according to family respondents.

An unmet need for vocational training was most commonly reported among the mildly retarded — nearly one-quarter of whom were not receiving training that families felt they needed. This may reflect higher expectations for the mildly retarded than for those who are moderately or severely retarded, or it may indicate that available training programs are simply not adequate to meet the demand for them among the mildly retarded.

Vocational skills represent a tremendous challenge to most mentally retarded persons for they are recognized as vital to an independent existence in the community. One mentally retarded person told an interviewer, *"I'd like to learn a trade. Like working in a hospital, making beds, working around the nurses with patients. Go to school and learn like nurses do."* Another said that he would like to learn *"to repair TV's and radios."*

Reading and writing were also frequently mentioned by retarded persons as skills they wanted to learn. One said, *"I would like to learn how to read a cookbook. If I could read, I could cook the food in there. The employees have to read it for me. I can put it in there and set the time and it comes out right. Ya, I would like to learn how to read."* Many felt vulnerable and dependent because of their poor reading skills; those who could read were often fiercely proud of this skill. One interviewer reported the following vignette:

> The client brought out his school papers and read all the numbers and all twenty of the words. They were "survival" words like police, help, fire, up, down, men, women, entrance, exit, etc. He then counted to 100 for me with not one hesitation or error. Because of this, I handed him a questionnaire for him to follow and he read each question out loud. I was extremely surprised. I'd say he was able to read correctly about 75 percent of the questions. He was so eager to read he could hardly wait till the next question.

Many family respondents expressed concern that so little progress had been made at the institution in acquiring reading and writing skills, whereas they were able to help the residents learn the basic words necessary for community life. In communities where public education for the retarded was unavailable, parents found themselves the sole resource for educational training, and many reported amazement at how difficult yet rewarding their efforts were. One field interviewer reported that a houseparent in a midwestern state used her days off to tutor residents in the group home.

DOMESTIC LIVING

About two-thirds of the study group received training in domestic living skills — housekeeping, meal preparation, shopping, and money management. Less than 10 percent of the study group were thought to be in need of such training but not receiving it. Less than half the children and the severely retarded received training in money management and shopping skills because they were not considered ready for it.

Discussions with retarded persons about taking care of their rooms or homes often provided a wealth of information on their individual proficiencies and interests. The following comments typify the kinds of domestic living skills learned:

> They taught me how to wax floors. I wish I knew how to fix furniture, like if a chair breaks, so I won't have to depend on someone else to fix it.

> I do take care of myself. I knew this when I was a kid. Shower, dress, feed, make my bed with no problems. I love to walk around, run errands.

> I know how to make my bed, shower, be neat, pick up. I match all my clothes. I don't mix plaids with flowers.

> They taught me how to run the washer and dryer. How to use an elevator.

> I worked in the dining room. I went to a home ec class. I learned to look at the menus to see what would be good to make. I worked on laundry and that taught me to do washing and drying. I mostly helped the other kids.

Many of the study group members wanted to learn money management skills; and several expressed the desire to have their own checkbook and bank statement. One person, when asked if there was anythink she would like to learn how to do, simply replied, "*Fill out a check, answer a telephone.*" Money management skills are often a prerequisite to being able to go on errands independently and learning to assume responsibility for oneself. One mentally retarded person told us, *"They should help me learn to subtract money — make change. I wish I knew how to use stores."* However great the desire for such training on the part of mentally retarded persons, their families often expressed concern that money management skills were extremely difficult to develop. In fact, over one-fifth of the study group (22 percent) were not considered ready for training in this area.

USE OF COMMUNITY RESOURCES

Less than half the study group received training in any of the skill areas in this category: travel skills (49 percent), use of the telephone (41 percent), learning to deal with emergencies (44 percent), and using community agencies (22 percent).

Many of the families indicated that the study group member was not ready for training in these areas; in fact, over half of the study group (55 percent) were not thought to be ready for training in using community agencies. About one-quarter of the group were not considered ready for training in using the telephone or learning how to cope with emergencies.

The skills needed for negotiating community life represent one of the most problematic areas of training. Many of the retarded persons spoke of their triumphs and fears concerning life in the community. One said, *"I can't live in the community on my own because I can't get around like regular people and it's hard to understand me."* Another said, *"As long as I'm on my own, I'd like to get an apartment on my own. I want to see more of the scenery outside. I don't feel like I'm shut in, but closed in — I feel like I want to feel more independent."*

On the other hand, some individuals were extremely successful in managing their lives in the community and using its resources. One interviewer wrote the following summary of a mentally retarded woman's experiences and capabilities:

> Ms. L. got her job at the Holiday Inn all by herself — her social worker just helped her to read the want ad in the newspaper. She shops for herself — and just bought a new bike and Polaroid camera. She keeps her own checkbook and writes her own checks and pays her own bills. She knows where to get what she wants and manages her day well. Ms. L. took drivers' training — now that says something for her capabilities in community life.*

---

* In the total study group, only 14 individuals had taken drivers' training and another four already had drivers' licenses.

One final indication of the ability to use community resources is voting behavior: 55 individuals, or 15 percent of the adults, were registered voters.

BEHAVIOR MANAGEMENT

As we mentioned earlier, behavior management was one of the most common types of training received. Nearly three-quarters of the study group received training in handling interpersonal relationships, controlling behavior, and participating in social and recreational activities. Both residences and community day or work programs provided this kind of training. Most of those who did not receive such training were said to have already developed good interpersonal skills.

One poignant remark by a retarded person illustrates the social dilemmas which can result from inadequate social skills. When asked what she wished she had been taught, she replied:

> *A few things like controlling my temper — getting along with other people — everyone I try working with, everywhere I go, people know I'm from the institution and from there they don't want my help because they think I'm crazy. You know, if I was crazy, I'd go to the hospital myself, but I'm not crazy — I don't tell people too much about myself.*

Another replied to a similar question, *"I would like to know how to be a wife."*

One characteristic noted by all interviewers was the mentally retarded person's desire to please the interviewer and to refrain from negative remarks. It was especially interesting that when asked what was a problem for them, many of the retarded respondents needed an explanation of the word "problem." This suggests that many do not differentiate between positive and negative experiences. Both their determination to learn how to get along with people and the considerable reinforcement they received for such skills were apparent: *"They taught me how to behave by getting after me. They got after me if I didn't get along."* Or, as another individual remarked, *"I learned how to get along with people. I learned to realize that other people have problems besides myself."*

SUMMARY

Numerous skills were being taught to the study group members in their communities, most commonly in the areas of personal maintenance, domestic living, and behavior management. Families and residential staff provided most of the training in these areas. Other types of training, such as learning how to negotiate community life (shopping, money management, coping with emergencies, dealing with community agencies, etc.), sensory development, and education and employment training were received less often. Community agencies and programs existing *outside* the home may be more likely to provide training in these areas. If so, the number of individuals who need these skills but are receiving little or no training in them provides some indication of the community's ability and willingness to support its mentally retarded population.

These patterns reflect the important role of families in providing training and services. Remember that for over 40 percent of the study group, the family acted as the community-based case manager, and was responsible not only for obtaining support services from other agencies, but also for providing various other types of services and training. On the average, one-fifth of the services and over half the training received by mentally retarded persons were provided by families. In fact, over two-thirds of the study group members were trained by their families in personal maintenance, domestic living, and community use skills.

These findings are somewhat distressing: the community residence was the single source for a wide range of care -- not unlike the institution. On the other hand, the findings can be interpreted positively as indicating that the homes to which the individuals were released perceived themselves as having a major and continuing responsibility for ensuring that the retarded person "made it" in the community. These families were not simply relying on others to ensure that the people in their care received appropriate services and training. Unfortunately, however, the burden was likely to be heaviest for the natural and foster families, since they received less outside support than the community residences and had less formal training in working with retarded people.

We also noted that severely retarded persons were more likely than mildly and moderately retarded individuals to be described as not yet ready for certain types of training. This could reflect an accurate assessment of severely retarded people's capabilities or it might indicate that families had lower expectations and provided fewer opportunities for them to develop new skills than in the case of the mildly or moderately retarded. Such a pattern could also reflect the absence of appropriate teaching strategies for the more severely retarded.

Chapter IX
How Well Are They Doing?

The preceding chapters have explored various aspects of the community experiences of study group members and their families. While many of these experiences were positive and successful, community living also presented problems for both the mentally retarded people and their families. These problems are important to highlight for they provide a sharp picture of the complex demands and challenges that the mentally retarded people and their families must meet in the community. This chapter presents information on three interwoven themes: the problems experienced in the community by both study group members and their families, the degree to which the members have adjusted to the central aspects of community living, and the concerns that they expressed about their new lives.

PROBLEMS LIVING IN THE COMMUNITY

At the most general level, there are three important elements of community life which may present difficulties for mentally retarded persons: employment, social behavior, and skills and support services. Families of study group members were asked whether or not the individual encountered problems in these three areas. (See Table IX.1.) The area most problematic for mentally retarded persons, according to family respondents, was employment: finding and keeping a job. Finding a job was either a big or moderate problem for about one-third of the study group, and keeping a job was a problem for over half the group. This may reflect economic uncertainties in many communities or it may indicate an absence of appropriate placements, support services, or training. Whatever the cause, job stability was noted by many families as a substantial problem.

Social behavior also entailed problems for mentally retarded persons, particularly in regard to family relationships, behavioral problems, and loneliness. The least problematic aspect of social behavior was staying out of trouble with the law.

The social interaction skills of mentally retarded persons thus continue to play an extremely important role in their ability to cope with community life. While services and training were described as fairly extensive in these areas (see Chapters VII and VIII), problems apparently persisted. Additionally, the fact that 40 percent of the families cited loneliness as a problem suggests that many of the study group members were isolated. They lacked either the opportunities for social interaction or adequate skills for developing stable relationships. As one mentally retarded person said, *"I'm lonesome all day, with no place to go, no one to talk to. I think only of myself. I got to get out of family care — it's getting on my nerves."*

Families noted fewer problems in the area of skills and service needs than in employment and social behavior. However, it should be noted that money management was either a large problem or somewhat of a problem for almost one-quarter of the study group. This difficulty has emerged throughout our discussions concerning training needs (see Chapter VIII) and was commonly voiced by mentally retarded persons themselves as a major obstacle to utilizing community resources.

Looking at the complete set of problems, an average of two-thirds of the families felt that the individual study group member was not having any difficulty in the three areas of employment, social behavior, and skills and support services.

Thus, many study group members were described as coping well with the demands of community life. This speaks favorably for both their ability to adapt to a new life in the community and the ability of their families to help in the adjustment process. However, the fact that job-related problems were the most commonly reported may indicate that in this area family support and/or social skills were not sufficient to ensure full integration into the community. These types of problems require more systematic and planned development of community resources to enable mentally retarded persons access to the full range of community experiences.

The mentally retarded study group members were also asked about their problems in the community.* The most striking difference between their responses and those of their families was that the mentally retarded persons were generally more likely to report problems than were their families (45 percent compared to 34 percent, respectively). (See Table IX.2.)

---

* Certain sensitive items were omitted from the list of problems which mentally retarded persons were asked about. Also, persons readmitted to institutions were not asked about their problems.

TABLE IX.1
FAMILY PERCEPTIONS OF STUDY GROUP'S PROBLEMS

Problem Area	Big Problem		Somewhat of a Problem		Not a Problem		Total	
	N	%	N	%	N	%	N	%
Employment[a]								
Finding a job	41	16	41	16	169	68	251	100
Keeping a job	84	26	89	28	147	46	320	100
Social Behavior								
Getting along at work or school	42	11	98	26	241	63	381	100
Family relationships	76	18	147	36	187	46	410	100
Behavioral problems	76	18	122	28	229	54	427	100
Loneliness	61	14	110	26	253	60	424	100
Staying out of trouble with the law	8	2	26	6	392	92	426	100
Socially unacceptable behavior	35	9	58	14	316	77	409	100
Developing self-confidence	30	7	76	18	323	75	429	100
Skills and Service Needs								
Medical problems	59	14	110	26	253	60	422	100
Self-care	31	7	106	26	273	67	410	100
Managing money	30	7	69	16	331	77	430	100
Getting help from community agencies	37	9	81	20	283	71	401	100
Average		12		22		66		

[a] Asked only about adults.

TABLE IX.2
STUDY GROUP'S PERCEPTIONS OF OWN PROBLEMS

Type of Problem	Big Problem		Somewhat of a Problem		Not a Problem		Total	
	N	%	N	%	N	%	N	%
Employment[a]								
Finding a job	37	17	75	34	110	49	259	100
Keeping a job	19	8	81	37	122	55	222	100
Social Behavior								
Getting along at work or school	21	7	106	37	160	56	287	100
Family relationships	19	7	92	34	159	59	270	100
Behavioral problems	22	8	106	40	140	52	268	100
Loneliness	37	13	111	38	144	49	292	100
Developing self-confidence	13	5	94	37	144	58	251	100
Skills and Service Needs								
Medical problems	16	6	87	31	171	63	274	100
Self-care	4	1	75	26	207	73	286	100
Managing money	37	14	113	43	110	43	260	100
Average		9		36		56		

[a] Asked only of adults.

Study group members were more likely than their families to feel that finding a job was a problem, perhaps reflecting the higher aspirations which study group members had for themselves. Many individuals expressed a desire for a better job which would pay them more, give them a greater feeling of accomplishment, and train them to accomplish more difficult tasks.

A more distressing and poignant finding is that study group members were considerably more likely than their families to feel that loneliness and lack of self-confidence were problems. Their sense of social isolation and inadequacy were perhaps not sufficiently recognized or appreciated by their families.

One mentally retarded person voiced her loneliness as follows, *"My mother frightens me. She's an alcoholic. I'm afraid she might try to kill herself. Nobody cares. I've had so much bad news this summer, but nobody cares."* Another remarked, *"I don't like nobody else. I don't have any friends."* A third person confided, *"I'm afraid of strange, new places, of getting lost or having no one to help me."* These statements may not be applicable to all mentally retarded persons; however, they do underline the fact that social isolation and feelings of inadequacy are serious problems for some.

Families were also asked about their own problems in dealing with the mentally retarded person in the home. A most common difficulty (reported by over half the families) was coping with the resident's behavioral and discipline problems. (See Table IX.3.) Stress on family relationships was another area in which considerable difficulty was noted by family respondents.

Many families also cited the inadequacy of community support services as a large problem. In particular, these services were needed to help locate social outlets and/or leisure activities and to meet educational and training needs. Lack of temporary relief services was noted as an additional problem for families.

ADJUSTMENT TO COMMUNITY LIFE

In general, both sets of respondents described study group members as adjusting very well to their new lives. (See Table IX.4.) In fact, families and study group members tended to voice remarkably similar assessments. In both cases, over three-quarters of the responses were positive; that is, indicating that the study group members were adjusting well to the home and to the community. Slightly less than two-thirds of the mentally retarded persons were perceived as adjusting well to the other residents in the home and to work and school.

TABLE IX.3
PROBLEMS FOR FAMILIES

Type of Problem	Big Problem		Somewhat of a Problem		Not a Problem		Total	
	N	%	N	%	N	%	N	%
Behavioral Problems								
Behavioral or disciplinary problems	85	22	128	33	176	45	389	100
Stress on family relationships	55	14	87	23	242	63	384	100
Meeting individual's psychological needs	36	9	66	17	288	74	390	100
Obtaining Support Services for Family								
Lack of temporary relief or respite care	26	10	28	11	209	79	263	100
Financial burden of caring for individual	27	7	37	9	325	84	389	100
Lack of other community support services for family	27	7	51	14	308	79	386	100
Obtaining Support/Training Services								
Meeting individual self-help needs	42	11	66	17	282	72	390	100
Meeting medical needs	12	3	34	9	344	88	390	100
Meeting educational/training needs	41	10	61	16	286	74	388	100
Finding leisure/social outlets for individual	52	13	105	27	231	60	388	100
Lack of other community support services	51	13	64	16	271	71	386	100
Lack of acceptance by community	17	4	61	16	311	80	389	100
Average		11		18		72		

TABLE IX.4
ADJUSTMENT TO COMMUNITY LIFE

Adjustment Category	Respondent	Very Well		All Right		Not Very Well		Total	
		N	%	N	%	N	%	N	%
Adjustment to the home	Family	317	73	85	20	30	7	432	100
	Study Group	232	73	61	19	25	8	318	100
Adjustment to other residents in the home	Family	274	66	99	24	44	10	417	100
	Study Group	192	63	85	28	27	9	304	100
Adjustment to work or school	Family	276	67	112	27	24	6	412	100
	Study Group	218	67	85	26	21	7	324	100
Adjustment to overall community life	Family	300	75	85	21	17	4	402	100
	Study Group	241	77	61	20	9	3	311	100

This pattern corresponds to the description of social relationships and job activities as somewhat problematic for mentally retarded persons.

WORRIES OF STUDY GROUP MEMBERS

When asked if anything worried them, about two-thirds of the study group members said no, indicating a fairly widespread sense of well-being among mentally retarded people living in the community. However, as Table IX.5 indicates, those who were troubled had fairly serious concerns. The most common worry (mentioned by 28 percent of the people) was a fear of being swindled or taken advantage of. One person vividly described this feeling of vulnerability: *"I'm afraid of all the things that are happening in the city. Getting raped, people getting killed, taking pills."* Another said, *"I was worried like when I was living by myself, until my roommate moved in, I was scared. Afraid that people will break into my house."*

The second and third most common concerns were loss of housing (20 percent) and being sent back to live in an institution (19 percent). One individual commented, *"I get nervous that I will be sent back to the institution because I'm not working."*

TABLE IX.5
WHAT WORRIES STUDY GROUP MEMBERS

Type of Worry	N	%
Being swindled/taken advantage of	136	28
Loss of housing	98	20
Being sent back to the institution	91	19
Being sick/having seizures	58	12
Loss of income	37	8
Crime (being robbed, etc.)	28	6
Getting lost	18	4
Not having or making friends	10	2
Hurting self or others	3	1
Total	479	100

SUMMARY

The problems faced by mentally retarded persons and their families are not significantly different from those faced by nonretarded persons. What does vary is the extent to which they are able to adjust to or cope with the consequences of these problems. For example, the problems most commonly reported by both the families and the study group members, were employment and behavioral difficulties. Social interactions appeared to be troublesome for many of the mentally retarded persons. Families reinforced this finding by noting that stress on family relationships was a problem for them in caring for a mentally retarded person. However, most study group members were described as making a very good adjustment to the community and to their new homes. Thus, there seems to be a fairly optimistic outlook for the future. As adjustment to new situations improves, and as families learn how to handle their newly returned or placed members, some of the other problems of loneliness and isolation may abate.

Study group members also expressed concerns about life in the community. Feelings of vulnerability were common. Learning to handle money, avoiding being swindled, making friends, and so forth were not only goals for many individuals, but also worries. These concerns highlight the need for supportive communities and families to ensure that mentally retarded persons are afforded the right to risk, as well as the right to live normally.

Chapter X
Who Is Returning to the Institution?

One of the most common ways of measuring the "success" of mentally retarded individuals who have been released to community settings has been to examine the rate of return to the institution. However, this approach avoids the complex reasons why some individuals do well in the community and others subsequently return. As we indicated in Chapter I, we were primarily interested in the experiences of mentally retarded people in the community — and these are particularly important to examine when trying to determine why some individuals return to the institution. The return may have been prompted by the individual's personal problems — such as severe psychological or behavioral difficulties which the community was unable to handle. Another factor may have been the family's or community's failure to provide adequate support services or activities for the mentally retarded person. Or perhaps the institution had not adequately prepared the individual for the transition to life in the community. Regardless of the reason, returning to the institution represents a type of "bottom-line" failure — on the part of the individual and the community — which warrants special attention. Therefore, in this chapter we review some of the major differences between the 58 study group members who returned to the institution and the 382 who remained in the community.

In regard to many of their individual characteristics, members of the two groups did not differ sharply. However, those who returned did tend to be less severely retarded. (See Appendix G, Table G.1.) About the same proportion of each group were adults (85 percent of those who returned and 80 percent of those who remained). (See Appendix G, Table G.2.) The most revealing differences emerged through comparisons of the individual qualities and community experiences of the two groups of mentally retarded persons. We will highlight six major differences in this chapter:

> Those who returned tended to be less severely retarded but were considerably more likely to have *behavioral or psychological problems* than those who remained.

> Those who returned were more likely to have been *living in foster homes*, both initially upon release from the institution and immediately prior to their return to the institution.

> They generally *participated in fewer community activities*, such as structured day programs (work or school), and spare-time and social activities.

> They tended to *have more unmet needs* for services and training.

> They tended to rely on *continued institutional support* while in the community.

> Those who returned were generally *less satisfied with living in the community*, and perceived themselves and were perceived by their families as adjusting less well in the community than individuals who remained.

It should be emphasized that these differences do not necessarily account for *why* people returned to institutions. The decision to go back to an institutional setting represents a judgment based on a series of interconnected conditions or experiences. For the purpose of this discussion, however, the major differences between the community experiences of those who returned and those who remained in the community are posited as possible explanations for the "success" of some and the "failure" of others.

BEHAVIORAL AND PSYCHOLOGICAL PROBLEMS

One of the most salient differences between the two groups was in the area of psychological problems. The ability of the community to handle behavioral problems can certainly influence whether or not the individual returns to the institution. Indeed, some study group members with behavioral problems remained in the community, and some of those who did not have such problems returned to the institution. Thus, it should not be assumed that the mere existence of a psychological problem was the reason for an individual's return to the institution.

How did the behavioral problems manifest themselves? First, those who returned were generally as likely as those who remained to have additional disabilities (other than mental retardation), but were considerably more likely to have psychological handicaps. Over one-half of the returning individuals were considered to have psychological disabilities, compared to 17 percent of those who remained. (See Table X.1.)

TABLE X.1

ADDITIONAL DISABILITIES AMONG THOSE WHO RETURNED
AND THOSE WHO REMAINED

Type of Disability	Returned		Remained	
	N(40)	%	N(248)	%
Psychological problems	22	55	41	17
Speech impairments	21	53	130	52
Mobility limitations	7	18	64	26
Epilepsy/seizures	8	20	50	20
Deafness or hearing impairments	5	23	36	15
Blindness or visual impairments	1	5	41	17

Second, those who returned were considerably more likely than those remaining in the community to have problems in their social and interpersonal relationships. (See Table X.2.) For about three-quarters of the former, according to their families, family relationships, behavioral difficulties, and loneliness constituted problems. About half exhibited socially unacceptable behavior and/or had difficulty getting along at school or work. While individuals who remained were not immune to these difficulties, fewer experienced them, and they appeared to be less severe when experienced.

Also, individuals who returned to the institution simply tended to have *more* problems than the other study group members. On the average, over half of the former had problems while less than one-third of the latter were described as experiencing various difficulties.

TABLE X.2
FAMILY PERCEPTIONS OF PROBLEMS IN THE COMMUNITY:
THOSE WHO RETURNED VERSUS THOSE WHO REMAINED

Problem Area	Big Problem				Somewhat of a Problem				Not a Problem				Total
	Returned		Remained		Returned		Remained		Returned		Remained		
	N	%	N	%	N	%	N	%	N	%	N	%	N
Jobs													
Finding a job	13	46	28	13	4	14	37	17	11	39	158	71	251
Keeping a job	13	30	71	26	9	20	80	29	22	50	125	45	320
Social Behavior													
Getting along at work (or school)	15	31	27	8	13	27	85	26	20	42	221	66	381
Family relationships	21	39	55	15	17	32	130	37	16	30	171	48	410
Behavioral problems	33	58	43	12	11	19	111	30	13	23	216	58	427
Loneliness	23	43	38	10	18	35	92	25	10	19	243	66	424
Staying out of trouble with the law	6	11	2	1	7	12	19	5	44	77	348	94	426
Socially unacceptable behavior	14	26	21	6	14	26	44	12	26	48	290	82	409
Developing self-confidence	8	15	22	6	3	5	73	20	44	80	279	75	429
Skills and Service Needs													
Medical problems	24	46	35	10	18	35	92	25	10	19	243	66	422
Self-care	11	20	30	8	22	40	84	23	22	40	251	69	420
Getting help from community services	9	16	21	6	18	32	51	14	30	53	301	81	430
Managing money	5	9	32	9	14	25	67	19	37	66	246	71	401
Average		30		10		25		22		46		68	

TABLE X.3
PROBLEMS FOR FAMILIES AMONG THOSE WHO RETURNED AND THOSE WHO REMAINED

Problem Area	Big Problem				Somewhat of a Problem				Not a Problem				Total
	Returned		Remained		Returned		Remained		Returned		Remained		
	N	%	N	%	N	%	N	%	N	%	N	%	N
Behavioral Problems													
Behavioral or disciplinary problems	33	57	52	14	6	16	119	31	12	21	164	43	386
Stress on family relationships	15	26	40	11	10	17	77	20	28	48	214	56	384
Meeting individual's psychological needs	17	29	19	5	11	19	55	14	26	45	262	69	390
Obtaining Supports for Family													
Lack of temporary relief	3	5	23	6	3	5	25	7	40	69	169	44	263
Financial burden of caring for individual	3	5	24	6	5	9	32	8	46	79	279	73	389
Lack of other community support services for family	5	9	22	6	8	14	43	11	39	67	269	70	386
Obtaining Support/Training Services for Individual													
Meeting self help needs	9	16	33	9	5	9	61	16	4	69	242	63	354
Meeting medical needs	1	2	11	3	3	5	31	8	50	86	294	77	390
Meeting educational/training needs	7	12	34	9	9	16	52	14	38	65	248	65	388
Finding leisure/social outlets for individual	9	16	43	11	14	24	91	24	31	53	200	52	388
Lack of other community support services	11	19	40	11	6	10	58	15	37	64	234	61	386
Lack of acceptance by community	4	7	13	3	9	16	52	14	41	71	270	71	389
Average		17		8		13		15		61		62	

Third, the behavioral difficulties of those who returned to institutions were more commonly a problem for their families than was true for families of individuals remaining in the community. (See Table X.3.) Behavioral and/or discipline difficulties were described as a big problem for over half the families of those who returned. In virtually all other problem areas, the differences between the two groups were slight, thus further highlighting the importance of behavioral problems among individuals returning to institutions.

Fourth, the major reason given by both individuals and their families for returning to the institution was behavioral problems. (See Table X.4.) As one individual explained, *"I came back because my mom and dad told me to go back. I stayed out late drinking and was late for work. I blew it — got in a fight with my boss."* Another said, *"I came because of my feet. I couldn't get around. My disposition probably wasn't so good either. Everything has changed."*

TABLE X.4
REASONS GIVEN FOR RETURN TO INSTITUTION

Reason	Family		Individual		Total
	N(32)	%	N(77)	%	N
Behavioral problems (at home, at work)	14	44	48	62	62
Lack of support services (housing, work, financial, medical)	8	25	18	23	26
Family readmitted the person for unspecified reasons	3	9	5	7	8
Other	7	22	6	8	13

In general, then, behavioral problems presented a considerable obstacle for many retarded persons. For some, the return to the institution may be attributable to the overwhelming nature of these problems as they affected families, work, school, social relationships, and, surely, themselves. For others, behavioral problems may not have been sufficiently severe to justify a return to institutional life. Certainly, the impact of psychological maladjustment on community experiences should be considered in relation to the other factors which we noted as differentiating those individuals who returned to the institution and those who remained in the community.

FOSTER HOME PLACEMENTS

The study group members lived in an assortment of residential settings in the community, most of which seemed to be positive environments. There were, however, specific differences between those who remained and those who returned in terms of the types of residences in which they lived while in the community. The biggest difference was in the proportion of foster home placements: 43 percent of the returning study group members had been living in foster homes immediately prior to readmission to the institution, compared with only 14 percent of those who had been placed in foster homes and who remained in the community. (See Table X.5.) This pattern also characterized initial placements upon release from the institution: 32 percent of those who returned compared to 11 percent of those remaining were initially placed in foster homes. (See Table X.6.) As a result of this difference, the former were somewhat less likely than the latter to have lived in all the other types of community settings.

As we discussed in Chapter VII, foster and natural homes tend to receive less support and be staffed by individuals with less formal education and training than other types of community residences. Foster homes are also likely to have different eligibility criteria — not only for the "parents" but also for the residents. There may actually be a tendency to place individuals with behavioral problems in foster homes rather than in other types of settings. Or, it is possible that the

TABLE X.5
RESIDENTIAL SETTINGS AMONG THOSE WHO RETURNED
AND THOSE WHO REMAINED

Type of Setting	Returned [a]		Remained		Total
	N(58)	%	N(382)	%	N
Natural/adoptive home	6	10	55	14	61
Foster home	25	43	53	14	78
Group home	21	36	188	49	209
Semi-independent living	4	7	40	10	44
Independent living	2	4	46	12	48

[a] The residential setting of those who returned refers to the type of residence lived in immediately prior to readmission to the institution.

TABLE X.6
INITIAL RESIDENTIAL SETTINGS UPON RELEASE
FROM THE INSTITUTION AMONG THOSE WHO RETURNED
AND THOSE WHO REMAINED

Type of Setting	Returned		Remained		Total
	N(56)	%	N(369)	%	N
Natural/adoptive home	6	11	47	13	53
Foster home	18	32	42	11	60
Group home	28	50	247	67	275
Semi-independent living	4	7	20	6	24
Nursing home	—	—	8	2	8
Independent living	—	—	5	1	5

people placed in foster homes are much the same as other retarded people, but that the foster homes are less able to handle them. Regardless, it is clear that all types of residential placements — and particularly foster homes — need to be examined carefully to determine their suitability for the types of individuals who are being placed in them, the kinds of support such homes must provide for residents, and the types of training needed by parents to care for their retarded charges.

LESS PARTICIPATION IN COMMUNITY ACTIVITIES

Those who returned and those who remained differed in terms of participation in a variety of community activities. One of the most striking differences was that nearly one-quarter of the study group members who returned to the institution were *not* involved in any day placement activity prior to readmission (compared to less than 10 percent of those who remained). (See Table X.7.) Nonparticipation in day placements may be a result of numerous factors; for example, individual behavioral problems, absence of appropriate placements in the community, or lack of appropriate skills for available placements. Regardless of the cause, the lower frequency of participation in day programs among individuals who returned to the institution surfaced as a rather obvious difference in their community experiences.

TABLE X.7
DAY PLACEMENTS AMONG THOSE WHO RETURNED
AND THOSE WHO REMAINED

Type of Placement	Returned [a]		Remained		Total
	N(69)	% [b]	N(512)	% [b]	N
Job (competitive or sheltered employment)	28	48	217	57	245
School (day or night classes)	14	24	157	41	171
Special day activity center or program	14	24	105	28	119
No school, work, or day activity program	13	23	33	9	46

[a] For those who returned, data refer to day placements prior to readmission to the institution.

[b] Percentages do not equal 100 because some individuals participated in more than one type of day activity.

Furthermore, those who returned tended to participate in fewer spare-time activities than those who remained. (See Table X.8.) Less than half of the former group played sports or attended sporting events, had hobbies, went out on dates, or attended club meetings. The fact that these represent some of the more active types of spare-time activities may suggest that those who returned were less likely to become involved in activities requiring some initiative and/or social interaction skills. Again, it should not be assumed that with increased participation in social activities these people would have remained in the community. Nevertheless, loneliness was cited by families of returning individuals as a major problem and we have also observed that lack of interpersonal competence was more prevalent among those who returned than among those who remained in the community.

One of the more striking aspects differentiating those who returned to the institution was their lack of friends in the community. (See Table X.9) While nearly all individuals remaining in the community had friends, 41 percent of those who returned were reported to have no friends while living in the community. Thus, individuals who returned to the institution appeared to be more lonely and less socially involved in the community than those who remained.

TABLE X.8
PARTICIPATION IN LEISURE ACTIVITIES
AMONG THOSE WHO RETURNED AND THOSE WHO REMAINED

Activity	Participates				Does Not Participate				Total
	Returned		Remained		Returned		Remained		
	N	%	N	%	N	%	N	%ᵃ	N
Watching TV, listening to radio	56	97	374	98	—	—	8	2	438
Shopping or errands	42	72	327	86	14	24	50	13	433
Movies	39	67	323	85	15	26	57	15	434
Vacations	30	52	321	84	26	45	56	15	433
Parties	34	59	293	77	21	36	87	23	435
Religious activities	31	53	276	72	23	40	98	26	428
Visiting friends	33	57	276	72	22	38	102	27	433
Playing sports	23	40	281	74	33	57	95	25	432
Hobbies	25	43	244	64	31	53	131	34	431
Attending sports events	16	28	235	62	40	69	141	37	432
Going on datesᵇ	14	24	96	25	39	66	252	66	401
Attending club meetings	7	12	74	19	48	83	306	81	435
Average		50		68		47		31	

ᵃ Percentages add to less than 100 because in some instances participation was not known by respondent.

ᵇ Asked only about individuals over 12 years old.

TABLE X.9
COMMUNITY FRIENDSHIPS AMONG THOSE WHO RETURNED
AND THOSE WHO REMAINED

Friendships	Returned		Remained		Total
	N(58)	%	N(382)	%	N
Has friends	34	59	380	99	414
Does not have friends	24	41	2	1	26

MORE UNMET NEEDS FOR SERVICES AND TRAINING

Among individuals who returned to the institution, the generally
lower level of participation in community activities (including day programs and leisure pursuits) and the greater likelihood of behavioral
problems are reflected in the fact that these people had more unmet
needs for specific types of services and training. (See Table X.10.)

TABLE X.10
UNMET SERVICE AND TRAINING NEEDS
AMONG THOSE WHO RETURNED AND THOSE WHO REMAINED

Services/Training Needed But Not Received	Returned %	Remained %
Services	12	6
Medical	9	8
Social/recreational	19	8
"Other"	7	3
Training	9	4
Personal maintenance	1	1
Sensory development	5	5
Education/employment	12	5
Domestic living	10	3
Community use	15	7
Behavior management	13	2

Overall, those who returned were twice as likely as those remaining in the community to have unmet service needs. Not surprisingly, the greatest difference between the two groups was in the area of social and recreational activities. (See Appendix G, Table G.3.) This was the type of service most often needed but not received by those who returned. However, in other areas, as well, persons who returned to the institution tended to use fewer services than the other study group members. On the average, only one-third of those who returned used each type of service, compared to almost half of those who remained.

Among individuals who returned to the institution, training was most often needed but not received in skills relating to use of community resources (getting around the neighborhood, using the telephone, coping with emergencies, and using community agencies), behavior management, and education or employment. These findings are particularly striking in light of the fact that those who returned were generally considered to have more skills than those who remained in the community. (See Appendix G, Table G.4.) Thus, although those who returned were thought to need less training than those who remained, the former were slightly more likely to need certain kinds of training they were not receiving, according to family respondents.

Training in personal maintenance and sensory development was generally either already sufficiently provided or unneeded by both groups of people. However, in terms of more advanced skills, those who returned were less likely than those who remained to have received training and were more likely to need it; this applies to training in education and employment, as well as in behavior management. This finding may well be related to other characteristics of those who returned to the institution — particularly, the fact that many lived in foster homes and did not participate in day activity programs. We found that foster homes tended to be less prepared than other residences to offer extensive training and that most training was provided by either families or day program staff. Thus, it is not surprising that a greater number of those who returned to the institution than those who remained in the community needed but did not receive training in advanced skills.

GREATER RELIANCE ON INSTITUTIONAL SUPPORT

Another interesting difference between the two groups is that those who returned were more likely to use institutional supports while living in the community. This is reflected in various ways. First, those who returned tended to receive institutional follow-up after their initial release. Second, institutional staff members were more likely to serve as case managers for those who subsequently returned. Third, almost one-quarter of the support services received by those who subsequently returned were provided by the institution.

Similarly, for those who returned to the institution there tended to be fewer community support services available and those which were offered tended to be used less often. While the differences are not dramatic, it appears that those who returned had fewer residential options in the community and that their families experienced slightly more difficulty in obtaining support services both for the mentally retarded person and for themselves. Overall, one-third of these families were dissatisfied with the community support services available, compared to a 10-percent rate of dissatisfaction among the families of those who remained in the community.

The implications of these findings are difficult to assess. From the outset, we noted that the role of the institution in the deinstitutionalization process has been the subject of much discussion (see Chapter II). The tendency among individuals who returned to the institution to receive more institutional and less community-based support and to have fewer residential options may suggest the need for more carefully planned and coordinated community-based programs of services and training. Conversely, these data perhaps underscore the importance of continuing to provide institutional services for individuals released to the community, as part of the total network of community support. Our findings do not resolve these issues conclusively.

LIVING IN THE COMMUNITY: LESS SATISFACTION AND POORER ADJUSTMENT

The pattern of community experiences differentiating those who returned to the institution and those who did not is perhaps best summarized by two disheartening findings: those who returned were less happy while living in the community and they made a poorer adjustment to living there, according to their families. These findings are not surprising considering the evidence of little participation in community activities, substantial loneliness, and numerous unmet needs for training in advanced skills among those who returned. Their expressed dissatisfaction in the community is presented here to highlight the fact that the "failure" to stay in the community was accompanied by frustration and, at times, ambivalence. One individual remarked, *"In family care you can't do what you want. They tell me what to do. I want to live on my own, have my own freedom."* Another said, *"I don't want to go back and forth. I want someone to treat me nice — go out with them. I don't like to stay alone."*

Dissatisfaction was expressed in both home and work experiences. (See Table X.11.) While virtually all individuals who remained in the community said that they liked their homes, less than half of those who returned expressed similarly positive sentiments. In fact, several were bitter and angry about their caretakers. One person said, *"They treated me mean. The foster mother yelled at me for no reason. She said I had nasty habits. There wasn't enough freedom."* Another noted, *"The house manager beat me up when I fed the dogs too much. I couldn't go anywhere. I had to stay in the house. Not allowed to open doors."* Over half of the people who returned said they preferred living in the institution to their previous community placement. Only 5 percent of those who remained in the community, however, said they would rather be back in the institution as opposed to staying in the community. However, many of those who subsequently returned to the institution had positive experiences in the community. In describing what they liked about their community homes, the following types of statements were common: *"The house was nice. I liked learning the house. I liked feeding the dogs. I liked going to the grocery stores, doing chores."* *"It was very nice — I had a bad seizure and hit my head, all bloody. That's what got me back to the institution. There was a mall across the street — got to go whenever I wanted. Everything was good."*

TABLE X.11
DISSATISFACTION WITH COMMUNITY EXPERIENCES
AMONG THOSE WHO RETURNED AND THOSE WHO REMAINED

Reason for Dissatisfaction	Returned %	Remained %
Dislike residence	43	10
Dislike work	46	35
Dislike school	10	10
Dislike day activity program	10	10
Have worries	46	31
Prefer institution to community placement	59	5

Dissatisfaction with community-based jobs was also more prevalent among those who returned. Almost half did not like their jobs, compared with about one-third of those remaining in the community.

TABLE X.12
FAMILY PERCEPTIONS OF ADJUSTMENT TO THE COMMUNITY:
THOSE WHO RETURNED AND THOSE WHO REMAINED

Adjustment Category	Very Well				All Right				Not Very Well			
	Returned		Remained		Returned		Remained		Returned		Remained	
	N	%	N	%	N	%	N	%	N	%	N	%
Adjustment to home	24	44	231	74	10	36	67	18	11	20	28	8
	(n = 55)		(n = 371)		(n = 55)		(n = 371)		(n = 55)		(n = 371)	
Adjustment to other residents in home	21	40	231	65	13	25	94	26	18	35	31	9
	(n = 52)		(n = 356)		(n = 52)		(n = 356)		(n = 44)		(n = 356)	
Adjustment to work or school	17	39	239	69	15	34	95	27	12	27	15	4
	(n = 44)		(n = 349)		(n = 44)		(n = 349)		(n = 44)		(n = 349)	
Adjustment to overall community life	30	63	250	73	15	31	76	22	3	6	17	5
	(n = 48)		(n = 343)		(n = 41)		(n = 343)		(n = 41)		(n = 343)	

TABLE X.13

STUDY GROUP'S PERCEPTIONS OF ADJUSTMENT TO THE COMMUNITY:
THOSE WHO RETURNED AND THOSE WHO REMAINED

Adjustment Category	Very Well				All Right				Not Very Well			
	Returned		Remained		Returned		Remained		Returned		Remained	
	N	%	N	%	N	%	N	%	N	%	N	%
Adjustment to home	21	47	236	75	11	24	56	18	13	29	21	7
	(n = 45)		(n = 313)		(n = 45)		(n = 313)		(n = 45)		(n = 313)	
Adjustment to other residents in home	17	42	207	67	15	37	79	26	9	22	21	7
	(n = 41)		(n = 307)		(n = 41)		(n = 307)		(n = 41)		(n = 307)	
Adjustment to work or school	18	49	200	70	13	35	72	25	6	16	15	5
	(n = 37)		(n = 287)		(n = 37)		(n = 287)		(n = 37)		(n = 287)	
Adjustment to overall community life	25	64	246	79	12	31	56	18	2	5	8	3
	(n = 39)		(n = 310)		(n = 39)		(n = 310)		(n = 39)		(n = 310)	

Both those who returned and those who remained expressed similar worries about living in the community. Many were particularly concerned about being swindled or taken advantage of. Others feared they would not be able to control their tempers. While these fears are not unusual for people to experience, they do represent a common thread in the lives of both groups of individuals — those who returned to the institution and those who remained in the community.

Adjustment to all aspects of community life was described as less positive for those who returned than for those who remained. However, families were slightly more likely than the individuals themselves to feel the adjustment to other residents in the home and to the house parents was poor. (See Tables X.12 and X.13.) Over one-third of those who returned were described by their families as adjusting poorly to other residents; while 20 percent were described as making a poor adjustment to the house parents.

SUMMARY

Individuals who subsequently returned to the institution in comparison to study group members who remained in the community, tended to be characterized by less participation in social activities, more unmet service needs and more ties to institutional supports. The overall assessment of their adjustment to community life tended to be poor. These indices provide fragmentary but helpful insights into the community experiences of those who returned to the institution as opposed to those individuals who remained in the community. There was no one "reason" why people returned to the institution, although behavioral problems were commonly cited as the critical factor.

In this chapter we have attempted to emphasize the diversity and complexity of people's experiences mainly by looking at their similarities. We hope that such an approach does not mask the wealth of individual differences, but that it does provoke further inquiry into the dimensions of a "successful" adjustment to community life.

Chapter XI
Coming Back:
Mentally Retarded People
and Their Families

Coming back to the community from an institution is a process which directly affects two groups of people: the retarded persons coming back, and the families to whom they come back. In preceding chapters we have presented an enormous amount of data covering many aspects of the community experiences of mentally retarded people, as reported both by the retarded individuals themselves and by their families. We have examined community experiences in terms of the specific components of the individual's life in the community. In this chapter we provide a more holistic view of the experiences of mentally retarded people and their families, in recognition of the fact that lives are not lived according to neatly separated categories.

One of the main challenges of this study was trying to capture the quality of coming back to the community. Coming back is above all a process — it takes time to adjust to new settings, people, expectations, and opportunities. It was particularly difficult to explore these experiences from a dynamic perspective because we collected data at only one point in time. We hope that the changing nature of the study group members' experiences has not been distorted by the fact that we "froze" their lives in this respect and artificially divided them into components of work, home, social life, and so forth. When we interviewed them, the retarded individuals were at different stages in the process of coming back to the community, encountering both ups and downs, problems and successes.

THE FAMILIES OF MENTALLY RETARDED PEOPLE

The family to which the mentally retarded person is released plays an extremely important role in the individual's community experiences. For the retarded person the residence provides a large proportion of the support services and training which are received in the community.

It is clear that the community residence often offers considerably more than simple "room and board" services. For many study group members, the parent (natural, foster or house staff) was the main case manager. Furthermore, the residence was not only responsible for *obtaining* supports from other agencies but was in fact a major *provider* of various types of services and training.

In certain respects these findings are somewhat distressing: the community residence appears to be functioning — not unlike the institution — as the single source of a wide range of care. In instances where community services are poor, the residence is virtually the only source of support for the retarded person. The diversity of care offered by the residences indicates that, in many ways, they are doing what institutions are often criticized for doing: meeting the total range of an individual's needs. To offer a more positive interpretation, the homes to which individuals are released tend to perceive themselves as having a major and continuing responsibility for ensuring that the retarded person "makes it" in the community. They do not rely totally on other agencies to meet the needs of the individual and frequently they provide continuity by extending the training and other supports offered in day programs and through community agencies. Whether one chooses the positive or the negative interpretation, the residence must be regarded as a crucial factor in the mentally retarded person's total experience in the community and as a potentially critical contributor to the success of coming back.

Despite the fact that families play such a central role in the community experiences of mentally retarded persons, they are frequently not receiving the amount of support which they need to carry out this important role. Many of the families felt that they had not been adequately prepared for the placement of the retarded person in the home. Professionally staffed residences tended to receive more preparation than natural or foster homes, but all types of families expressed a strong need for this type of support. Since for many persons natural families may be the most desirable community placement, it is disturbing that this gap in service exists. A similar lack of supports may well have contributed to the natural family's initial decision to institutionalize their child.

THE MENTALLY RETARDED PEOPLE

A unique aspect of this study was the fact that we interviewed the mentally retarded persons themselves to obtain their perspective on coming back. Too often, studies have gathered information only from those who work with or care for these people. Although such insights are indeed valuable, the opinions of the mentally retarded persons are equally essential to forming a complete picture of the community experiences of deinstitutionalized mentally retarded persons. Indeed, who would know better what these experiences have been and have meant to them?

Most of the people released into community settings expressed basically positive feelings about coming back. On the whole, they were satisfied with their homes and their school or work placements. And they strongly preferred living in the community to returning to the institution.

Although generally positive about their experiences, study group members offered many insights into their problems and the inadequacy of supports for them, both at the institution and in the community. They had a keen sense of their own needs -- for training in community living skills, for help in managing behavioral problems and family relationships, for opportunities to socialize and develop friendships. They had a good sense of their strengths and accomplishments as well. They were intensely proud that they were "making it" in the community — that they held jobs, earned salaries, learned new skills, lived in their own rooms, owned their own televisions, cooked for themselves, went on dates. As one study group member proudly related: *"I'm doing real good in the community. I'm doing my best anyhow."*

Study group members had high aspirations for themselves:

I'd like to pick my own job. I'd like to be a trucker.

I'd like my own apartment if I was old enough.

I'd like to get along with people and do well.

I would like to go to school at night from 6:30 to 8, five nights a week, so I can learn to read and multiply.

Because of their aspirations, they were not always content with their current situations. They wanted better jobs, better salaries, training in more advanced skills, more social outlets. Underlying these aspirations was a strong desire for freedom and the opportunity to live a normal life — to live in their own homes with people of their own choice, to have privacy, to have friends and an active social life, to get married, to have children, to have decent jobs.

The desire for freedom to make their own decisions and to have control over their lives is reflected in numerous comments by study group members. Many persons were impressed with their newly acquired freedom in the community:

> *I like living here. More freedom — go shopping, go downtown, go to movies. We go places.*

> *I like to get out 'cause it's more freer and there are a lot more things to do.*

> *I can go shopping anytime I want to. I think I have more freedom here than at the institution. I get to meet different people.*

> *Well, I can have company as long as I want to — they don't have to leave at a certain time. I like to watch the "FBI" and "Creature Feature" and that's on late at night. And I can go out with a girlfriend or boyfriend and come home when I want. I can come home when I want.*

> *I can do what I want: I can paint pictures, sew, do own cooking, go to bed early. Go outside when I want to, not be locked in. Had enough of that.*

Others, however, did not feel that they were allowed to do enough on their own.

In many instances in this study, there were discrepancies between the expectations of families and those of the study group members. Families tended to have lower expectations of the mentally retarded person's capabilities in regard to training, employment, and special activities. This was particularly true in the case of families of severely retarded persons. Although severely retarded persons encountered many problems in school, work, and social life, their families tended to be satisfied with these experiences — perhaps because they expected very little of the severely retarded.

Some people might argue that the aspirations of the study group members were unrealistically high. Yet we found these people to be extremely accurate in their perceptions. In many instances, when the same question was asked of both the families and the study group members, the responses were remarkably similar. Both groups cited similar problems in community living and gave similar ratings of the individual's management of personal relationships and overall adjustment in the community.

Perhaps our most important finding was that mentally retarded persons are able to speak for themselves — accurately and poignantly. Members of the study group were able to provide us with a complex and moving account of their experiences in coming back to the community. In many ways, the experiences which they described were not unique — they did not differ from the kinds of experiences one would expect of "normal" people in the community. Study group members spent time in their homes, went to work or school, watched TV, went shopping. Like most people, they were content with some aspects of their lives but dissatisfied with others. They encountered certain problems and tried hard to cope with them. Above all, these people were in the process of changing — adjusting to new homes and communities, acquiring new skills, making new friends, confronting new problems. Perhaps this is why it is so difficult to summarize or characterize their lives.

It is the aspect of change which is perhaps most striking about members of the study group. Many of them had come a long way from the institution to the community in terms of their experiences. And their journeys were not over. As one study group member responded when asked by the interviewer if she would be willing to participate in a possible follow-up study a year later, *"Yes. I'll still be here. I'll be a little older and a little wiser, but I'll still be here."*

Appendices

Appendix A
Study Methodology

OVERVIEW

The research design employed in the study upon which this book is based consisted of four phases: conceptualization, instrument design data collection, and analysis and report writing. (See Figure A.1.) These phases are briefly described below and discussed in more detail in the following sections.

Based on the findings of a review of the literature, we developed a conceptual model of the processes of deinstitutionalization and community adjustment in the first phase of the study. The model presented our assumptions about these processes* and included nine sets of variables encompassing the major characteristics of deinstitutionalization and community adjustment experiences.

The second phase consisted of instrument design. We developed three groups of instruments to collect data on the nine variable sets:

Institutional Mail Questionnaire (IMQ) — a mail questionnaire designed to obtain information on the deinstitutionalization procedures and release patterns of 250 institutions across the nation serving mentally retarded clients.

Deinstitutionalization Procedures Questionnaire (DPQ) — a questionnaire designed to survey ten institutions selected for in-depth case study descriptions regarding deinstitutionalization and prerelease policies, procedures, and programs.

"Family" Questionnaires (FAMQ) — a series of instruments designed to obtain data on the community experiences

---

* Reported in Volume I of the Final Report of the study. Copies of the Final Report can be obtained from Abt Publications.

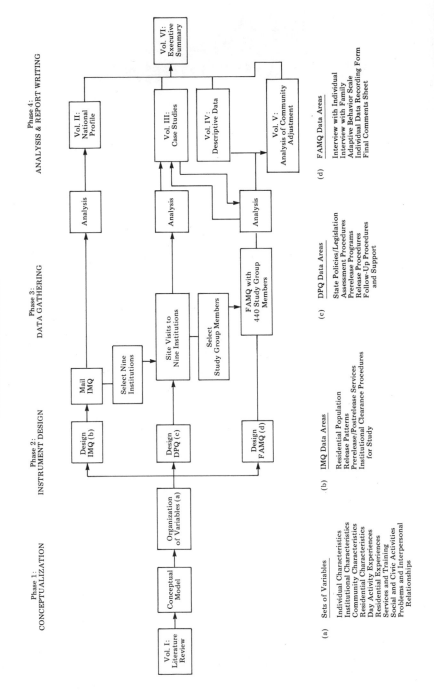

Figure A.1
OVERALL RESEARCH DESIGN

of deinstitutionalized persons living in the community. The instruments included an interview questionnaire to be administered to the deinstitutionalized person; a questionnaire administered to the person's family; an Adaptive Behavior Checklist (ABS) measuring the functional level of the person; a Client Data Recording Form (CDRF) obtaining demographic data from institutional records about the person (e.g., age, number of years institutionalized, date of discharge, etc.); and a Final Comments Sheet (FCS) to record interviewer's impressions.

During the third phase of the study we administered the three sets of instruments described above to the appropriate respondents in a sequential fashion. First, the IMQ was mailed to 250 institutions serving persons across the nation. Nine institutions were selected for in-depth case study descriptions. The nine institutions were then visited by project staff who collected data using the DPQ. Based on the data they obtained and on further contact with institutional staff, 440 deinstitutionalized persons released from the nine institutions were selected for study. Finally, the FAMQ series of instruments was used to gather data on study group members.

The data were analyzed and reported during the fourth phase of the study. The IMQ data results were reported in *Volume II: Profile of National Deinstitutionalization Patterns, 1972-1974.*

The data obtained from the DPQ were analyzed in two ways. First, case study descriptions of the individual institutions and a cross-case study summary were reported in *Volume III: Case Studies of the Deinstitutionalization Procedures of Ten Selected Institutions Serving Mentally Retarded People.* Second, portions of the DPQ data served as predictor variables for the analysis reported in *Volume V: An Analysis of Factors Associated With Community Adjustment.*

Similarly, the FAMQ data were analyzed in several ways. Data on the community experiences of persons in the study group were described in *Volume IV: Descriptive Data on the Community Experiences of Mentally Retarded Persons* and also in the final chapter of each of the case study descriptions of the institutions contained in Volume III. FAMQ data were also organized into predictor and outcome measures of community adjustment and reported in *Volume V: An Analysis of Factors Associated With Community Adjustment.* All of the data collected and reported in the five volumes were then analyzed in terms of their implications for overall study findings and recommendations. The results of this final analysis and our recommendations were reported in *Volume VI: Executive Summary.*

CONCEPTUALIZATION

The purpose of the first phase of the study was to develop a conceptual model for assessing the community experiences of deinstitutionalized persons. First, we reviewed the literature to become acquainted with previous work in this area. Persons currently conducting similar research were contacted by telephone or in person and asked to describe their projects. We then reviewed the information obtained from these sources to determine its relevance to the current study.

As a result of the information obtained from the literature search and the practical experience and knowledge of Abt Associates staff about the deinstitutionalization process, we identified the major research question of this study:

> What are the major institutional, community, and individual variables which contribute to the successful community experiences of deinstitutionalized mentally retarded people?

We then developed a conceptual model of community experiences to address this question. The purpose of the model was both to set forth the study's assumptions about the process of deinstitutionalization and community experiences, and to help us organize the sets of outcome and predictor variables around which the instrument design, data collection, and data analysis phases were organized.

Study's Assumptions Regarding Deinstitutionalization and Community Experiences

One of the major findings of the literature review was that the terms "deinstitutionalization" and "community experiences" have been widely used and connote different meanings and values in various contexts. It was therefore essential to define these terms and clarify our use of them in the study's conceptual model.

Deinstitutionalization has traditionally referred to the preparation of institutionalized persons for release into community settings, and their subsequent release. For the purposes of the study, we defined *deinstitutionalization* as the placement of mentally retarded people in community settings following their enrollment in residential institutions (facilities serving over 100 handicapped persons) for two or more consecutive years. *"Community placements"* or *settings* include natural homes, foster homes, group homes, and semi-independent as well as independent living units. Specifically excluded were residential settings which were restrictive or as sheltered as the institutions from which individuals were released (e.g., nursing homes, state schools, and state hospitals) and residences serving over 100 persons. A mentally retarded person was considered deinstitutionalized if he or she was residing in the community (i.e., sleeping in the community residence and using it as a mailing address), regardless of whether or not that person was receiving support services at the institution from which he or she was released.

The community experiences described in this book reflect an interactive process in which an individual adapts over time to the community environment in which he or she lives, works, studies, and so forth. The time and budget constraints of the study, however, limited the extent to which these experiences could be measured. Thus, we did not measure experiences in the community across two or more time periods — rather, data was collected only at one point in time. Also, we focused almost exclusively on the adaptive behaviors of the individuals to the various contexts and settings in which they live, and did *not* attempt to examine these settings' adaptation to the demands and needs of the individual.

Organization of Variables

We compiled a list of variables related to deinstitutionalization and community experiences, guided by the major research question and the theoretical assumptions of the study. Variables were organized into two major sets: (1) outcome variables, or measures of community experiences; and (2) predictor variables, which impact on the community experiences. The predictor variables dealt with individual characteristics and experiences *prior to* release to community settings, and outcome variables described community experiences *since* release into the community.

Three subsets of predictor variables were analyzed in terms of their relationships to four subsets of outcome variables. The *predictor variables* included the following subsets:

Subject Variables — characteristics of the deinstitutionalized mentally retarded persons (e.g., age, sex, intelligence level, functional level).

Community Variables — characteristics of the community settings in which individuals are placed (e.g., types and size of settings, proximity to shopping and transportation services).

Institutional Variables — characteristics of the institution itself (e.g., size, per capita expenditures, staff/client ratios) and of the study group members' former institutional experiences (e.g., training, work, school, and social activities).

The major *outcome variables* were organized into four subsets:

Day/Residential Experiences — data related to experiences in day and residential placements in the community (e.g., types of placements, satisfaction with placements).

Services and Training — data on types and frequency of services and training received by individuals (and families) since release from institution.

Social and Civic Activities — data on types of activities and frequency of participation by clients since release from the institution (e.g., leisure activities, friendships).

Problems and Interpersonal Relationships — data on individual and family perceptions of the study group members' management of interpersonal relationships with others in the community (e.g., other program participants, staff, and other residents); the types of problems encountered by study group members and their families.

Limitations in Developing the Conceptual Model

A major limitation in developing the conceptual model was the small amount of theoretical and empirical work previously accomplished in this area. The literature review revealed that there is little information available about the community experiences of deinstitutionalized persons, and few, if any, relationships have been established between specific community experiences and the deinstitutionalization process. Because a body of knowledge has not yet been established in this area, it is possible that we have overlooked some important aspects in designing our conceptual model.

Although the variables we selected cover a broad range of issues related to the deinstitutionalization process and community experiences, certain types of variables were excluded. Some would have been too difficult to collect, given the time period and scope of the project. For example, variables potentially related to community experiences, such as the self-esteem of deinstitutionalized people or community acceptance of them are extremely difficult to measure. Also, certain areas, such as sexual and legal problems, were considered too sensitive in nature, and potentially offensive to individuals to be included in interview questionnaires. Finally, we excluded variables not relevant to our basic focus on activities of the study group members. For example, detailed data on the nature of the group homes to which persons were released, although equally interesting, were not identified as relevant to this study.

INSTRUMENT DESIGN

Design of the Institutional Mail Questionnaire (IMQ)

A questionnaire was designed and mailed to approximately 250 institutions identified by the National Center for Health Statistics as serving mentally retarded people. The form was kept brief to encourage responses. Its purposes were twofold: (1) to provide data on institutions which would enable the project staff to select nine institutions for participation in the study of community experiences of deinstitutionalized mentally retarded persons; and (2) to provide data for developing a national profile of deinstitutionalization patterns. Beyond providing information on these patterns, the profile would become a base for comparison of the information gathered on the ten institutions chosen for further study.

Data were gathered on the following topics: number of clients served by the facility; number released to various types of community settings; age and level of retardation of individuals placed in various community settings; types of prerelease and postrelease services available; and institutional approval procedures required to contact released individuals about the study.

Design of the Deinstitutionalization Procedures Questionnaire (DPQ)

The Deinstitutionalization Procedures Questionnaire (DPQ) was developed by project staff to collect information on two major sets of variables: (1) those required to produce descriptive case studies on the deinstitutionalization policies and procedures of the nine facilities; and (2) those necessary to analyze factors contributing to postrelease community experiences.

The majority of the questions in the DPQ were closed-ended to facilitate coding and use of the variables in the analysis of community experiences. Open-ended questions were reserved for variables used only in the case study descriptions. We pretested the questionnaire at institutions for the mentally retarded in two states in order to refine the questions, estimate the time involved in conducting interviews, and determine appropriate respondents. The questionnaire was subsequently revised on the basis of these pretests.

A major limitation of the DPQ was that it provided data on deinstitutionalization only from the institutions' perspective. No information was obtained on the views of other interested parties, such as community representatives, consumers, or state officials. In addition, the DPQ dealt only with institutional characteristics presumed to relate directly to deinstitutionalization; thus, no general overview of the characteristics of the institutions was provided.

Design of the Community Questionnaires

Variations in the types of settings of persons and their families necessitated the design and use of setting-specific questionnaires for the community interviews. In each case, the family of the person was interviewed first.* If possible, the mentally retarded individual was interviewed separately from the family.

Table A.1 specifies the types of data collected in each of the instruments. The various questionnaires used with different types of families were quite similar; they differed only in respect to certain questions specific to the particular setting. For example, in the Natural Parent Questionnaire, certain questions were asked about parent and sibling relationships with the study group member, whereas in the Housemanager's Questionnaire, questions were asked about the staffing patterns in the group home and about the study group member's relationship with the staff.

In addition to these questionnaires, the following instruments were used to gather information about each member of the study group:

Adaptive Behavior Scale (ABS) — information provided by the family or contact person about the individual's current level of functioning in a variety of domains (e.g., social, vocational, physical, personal). This standardized scale is published by the American Association on Mental Deficiency and has been used in many related studies in this field.

Final Comments Sheet (FCS) — a series of observational scales and impressionistic data filled out by the interviewer after the interview was completed. FCS data included the interviewer's impressions of the individual's experiences, satisfaction, and social integration; the individual's overall appearance (demeanor, cleanliness, dress); the physical condition of the home and setting; as well as information on the conduct of the interview.

Client Data Recording Form (CDRF) — demographic information about the individual provided for this study by the institutions from their records. CDRF data included age, sex, race, level of retardation, number and length of institutionalizations, commitment and discharge status, and participation in prerelease programs.

---

*"Families" is used here to refer to the deinstitutionalized individual's natural parent(s), foster parent(s), or guardian(s); group home housemanager(s); or any other person(s) who provided care and supervision in the residential setting. In cases where deinstitutionalized persons were living independently, a contact person from the community (such as a social worker assigned to the individual) was interviewed as well.

TABLE A.1
TYPE OF DATA COLLECTED BY EACH INSTRUMENT

Instrument	Data Collected
Resident Questionnaire	Respondent's satisfaction with residence; satisfaction with day placement (work, school, etc.); major problems since leaving institution; skills learned in institution to prepare respondent for living in the community; skills which *could have* been taught at institution to prepare for community living; skills acquired by respondent since living in the community; skills which respondent wants to learn in the community.
Returnee Questionnaire	Information about respondent's community experience paralleling Resident Questionnaire data.
Family Questionnaire (basically the same for natural parents, foster parents, group home staff, and semi-independent living staff)	Background information on family respondent's relationship to and contact with the study group member, background information on the study group member, skills learned in the institution; skills needed for living in the community; community services used/or needed by the study group member and the family respondent; information about day placement (school, work, etc.), spare-time activities, socialization in the community, and community adjustment.
Independent Living Questionnaire	All information in Resident Questionnaire plus most of the information about community experiences contained in Family Questionnaires.
Questionnaire for Contact Person of Resident in Independent Living Setting	Background information on respondent's relationship to and contact with the study group member; respondent's perception of study group member's community adjustment; skills learned in the institution; skills needed to learn to live in the community.

Very little was known about the most effective structuring of questions to be used in interviewing mentally retarded people at the time of the study. The reliance on closed-ended questions may have resulted in too narrow a range of responses. Open-ended questions were used occasionally in the questionnaires administered to study group members when the range of possible responses was unknown or unpredictable. However, in asking these open-ended questions, we may have erred in the opposite direction; that is, obtaining a range of responses too broad to aggregate and code.

Selection of Institutions

Our initial list of 250 institutions was obtained from a national directory of institutions serving mentally retarded persons, provided by the National Center on Health Statistics. The Institutional Mail Questionnaire was mailed to these 250 institutions in the fall of 1974; 154 of them responded.

Of those institutions responding to the Institutional Mail Questionnaire, we identified 26 which met the following four screening criteria:

> The institution had to be residential and serve at least 100 persons. *Rationale:* The cutoff point of a minimum of 100 clients was selected to correspond with the definition of institution used in this study.

> The institution must have deinstitutionalized (i.e., released to community settings) at least 50 mentally retarded persons between the ages of six and 40, who had been enrolled in the institution for two or more years prior to release, since January 1, 1972. *Rationale:* In order to obtain a sample of approximately 500 deinstitutionalized persons, it was imperative that each of the institutions selected had released at least 50 individuals. (The criteria regarding age, length of stay in institution, and date of release are listed below in the description of procedures for selection of the study group.)

> The institution must have maintained a list of the *current* addresses or telephone numbers of released persons. *Rationale:* Since the procedures for obtaining a sample of deinstitutionalized individuals were dependent on the accuracy of the institutions' files on released persons, only institutions which claimed that they had current addresses and telephone numbers of released individuals were included.

> The clearance procedures for obtaining consent for the institution to participate and to contact deinstitutionalized individuals could not exceed four to six weeks. *Rationale:* Each institution indicated through the mail survey the specific clearance procedures necessary for them to participate (e.g., review and approval by institutional officials, state officials, or human rights commissions). Because of the time

constraints of this project, only those institutions which anticipated clearance within four to six weeks were included in the institutional study group.

Of the 26 institutions meeting the above criteria, nine were selected using the following guidelines:

At least five states had to be represented to ensure geographical diversity.

A wide range of deinstitutionalization processes had to be represented, so that the case studies would be as varied and informative as possible.

States with different types of Right to Education Laws had to be represented, since this might be an important potential variable in the community experiences of mentally retarded persons.

The institution had to be willing to participate. The study was voluntary and could obviously include only those institutions which consented to participate.

Three basic limitations were imposed on the data by the process of selecting the institutions. First, the initial group of institutions which responded to the mail survey was a self-selected sample. It is not impossible to determine whether the institutions which responded differed from those which did not, since no data on nonrespondents were available.

Second, the four screening criteria used to limit the pool of 250 institutions to 26 further restricted the types of institutions included. To meet our criteria, they had to be relatively large; they had to have released a fairly large number of individuals to community settings; they had to maintain records on the whereabouts of these individuals; and they had to have relatively simple clearance procedures. The 26 institutions selected may well differ from the others which were eliminated during the screening process.

Third, the final selection of the nine institutions was influenced by the willingness of institutions to participate. Two of the nine initially selected refused to participate, and had to be replaced by other institutions from the pool of 26. One of the institutions refused because of concern about the amount of work involved in participaton; another because of recent major administrative staff changes at the institution. The institutions consenting to participate may differ from those which refused. Thus, these selection procedures limit the extent to which the study findings can be generalized. No definitive statements can be made regarding whether or not the nine institutions selected for study are representative of the universe of institutions serving mentally retarded persons. By the same token, there is no reason to assume that the nine institutions are unique. A detailed description of the institutions is provided in Volume III of the Final Report.

Selection of the Study Group

Selection of study group members from the institutions was based on four criteria.

The individual must have lived in the institution for two or more years. *Rationale:* This requirement was intended to control for the confounding effect of brief institutional stays on assessment of community experiences.

An individual must have been released from the institution to a community placement. *Rationale:* Since the goal of this study was to assess the *community* experiences of persons released from institutions, it was important to define community placements carefully. We defined natural homes, foster homes, group homes, and semi-independent and independent living settings as community placements. Our definition excluded residential settings which were as large, restrictive, or sheltered as the institutions from which the individuals were released; excluded were state schools and hospitals, nursing homes, and residential settings serving over 100 persons.

An individual must have been between the ages of six and 40 years at the time of release. *Rationale:* The age range was selected in consultation with the Bureau of Education for the Handicapped. The number of children under the age of six who met the criterion of two years of institutional experience prior to community placement, would have been too small to be analytically useful for this study. Persons over the age of 40 were excluded because many of them were released to nursing or convalescent care settings which did not meet our definition of community placement.

An individual must have been released from the institution between January 1, 1972 and December 31, 1974. *Rationale:* The time period for release was chosen in consultation with the Bureau of Education for the Handicapped.

Projections indicated that a three-year period would be necessary to obtain a sample of 500 released individuals. A person was considered "released" if he or she resided in the community (i.e., slept in a community residence and used it as a mailing address), and if he or she was explicitly considered to be living outside the institution either permanently or on a trial basis.

Confidentiality and Consent

In order to ensure that the privacy of all study group members was protected, we asked participating institutions to make initial contact with the individuals. Abt Associates developed a standard letter describing the study, detailing what participation by the individual and his or her family would entail, and requesting that they sign and return an enclosed consent form.

The consent form, developed by a legal consultant experienced in the field, was written in a style which could be understood by mentally retarded persons and/or their families. Individuals signing the form gave consent both to participate in the study and to allow the releasing institutions to provide basic information about them (e.g., level of retardation, number of years institutionalized). Legal consent was furnished by the parent or guardian if the individual was a minor or was judged legally incompetent. If neither a minor nor judged incompetent, the mentally retarded person was required to sign the consent agreement.

The consent forms were sent to the nine institutions which took responsibility for mailing them to eligible released individuals. Mentally retarded persons and their families were instructed to return the signed consent form directly to Abt Associates if they were interested in participating in the study. In this way, Abt Associates did not make any direct contact with the study group members and their families until after they had agreed to participate; and researchers never learned the names of those who declined to partipate. Thus, the privacy of both respondents and nonrespondents was ensured.

Response Rate of Sample

The participating institutions released a total of 1,242 individuals who met the criteria for selection noted above. Of these, 919 were living in the community and 323 had subsequently returned to the institution (i.e., the latter were released between 1972 and 1974 but had since returned to the institution). Only 296 of the 919 individuals living in the community agreed to participate in the study.

A second mailing resulted in an additional 101 individuals consenting to participate. Thus, as a result of both mailings, 397 individuals living in the community agreed to participate — amounting to 43 percent of the total sample of 919 individuals in the community.

We decided also to interview individuals who had returned to the institution, thereby obtaining valuable information on a subset of persons who failed to adjust to the community, according to at least one criterion for success — remaining in the community. Eighty-three (83) individuals agreed to take part — or 26 percent of the total sample of individuals who had returned to the institution.

Ninety-five (95) envelopes never reached their destination because of faulty addresses. In addition, three persons were eliminated from the sampling pool because they did not meet the selection criteria (e.g., they were living in nursing homes or they had never in fact been released from the institution). Thus, 1,144 persons were actually contacted as a result of the first mailing.

The sample totaled 480 persons (397 living in the community and 83 who had returned to the institution) — constituting 42 percent of the 1,144 people contacted. It should be noted, however, that the final sample size decreases slightly as a result of unavoidable contingencies in the field (such as individuals deciding at the last minute that they did *not* want to participate) and conflicting vacation schedules. Taking these changes into account, the final study group consisted of 440 individuals, or 35 percent of the 1,242 persons initially identified by the institutions.

Several aspects of this selection process limit the extent to which data about the study group can be generalized. First, the selection criteria and the definition of "study group member" were in some ways arbitrary. For example, we could have used a one-year residence requirement in the institution and/or established a wider (or narrower) age range. There is, of course, no way of knowing the effect of the selection criteria on the composition of the sample and the ensuing results.

Second, participation was voluntary. It is impossible to determine whether persons consenting to participate differed from nonrespondents since no information was obtained about persons who did not respond or who decided not to participate.

Third, it is possible that the final sample is biased toward persons who did not frequently change residence after release. Because of changed or incorrect addresses, 95 individuals never received the letter. It is difficult to know whether these persons differed from the final sample.

Finally, the sample may underrepresent individuals placed in certain types of settings and overrepresent people in other settings. For example, it is possible that proportionately more people placed in group homes and natural families elected to participate because they were living with or supervised by persons who could encourage them to respond to the request and assist them in doing so. On the other hand, persons living in independent settings may be underrepresented because there was no one in their immediate setting who could offer similar help.

DATA GATHERING

Gathering Data on the Institutions

The Institutional Mail Questionnaire was mailed in the fall of 1974 to 250 institutions across the country serving mentally retarded persons. A follow-up mailing took place in December 1974. All institutions which did not respond were telephoned during January and February 1975 to find out why they had not responded and encourage them to do so. As a result of these data collection efforts, 154 institutions responded to the IMQ.

Each of the nine institutions participating in the study was visited by a research team. The objectives of the site visits were three-fold. First, the visits were intended to gather data necessary to produce descriptive case studies on the deinstitutionalization procedures and policies of each facility. A second objective was to gather data on characteristics of the institution identified as possible predictor variables for factors contributing to successful community experiences. A third purpose of the visits was to review with the institutional staff the proposed procedures for contacting the deinstitutionalized persons and for gathering information about them from the institutional case records.

Four interviewers from Abt Associates who were experienced in interviewing staff in programs for the mentally retarded visited and administered the DPQ at the nine sites. The DPQ respondents varied at each site; in most cases, the superintendent of the institution participated, as well as other staff who could provide the information requested in the questionnaire. For example, the Director of Social Services or Community Placement (where such positions existed) responded to items in that area. Interviewers were instructed to record staff responses to each questionnaire item in an effort to collect information which could later be reported in a descriptive case study.

It generally took six to eight hours to gather the information for the DPQ and to review the proposed procedures for contacting the study group members.

This procedure limited the data gathered in several respects. First, the case studies were intended to be primarily descriptive, not evaluative. Moreover, the interviewers merely recorded information provided by institutional staff. Because of time and budget constraints, no effort was made to verify the accuracy of the information. Thus, the reliability and accuracy of the institutional data collected might be questioned.

Second, although the questionnaire and data requirements of the DPQ were mailed to each institution in advance of the site visit, many institutions had difficulty in providing the requested demographic data. Often, the staff felt their records were inaccurate or out of date. In cases where exact figures could not be provided, respondents were asked to give their best estimates.

Third, the DPQ was administered at each site to only a small number of respondents, usually the superintendent of the institution and one to three other key staff members. No attempt was made to interview *all* the institutional staff or to obtain a representative view of the deinstitutionalization policies and procedures at the facilities. Therefore, the data collected may represent only a limited perspective.

Finally, the DPQ was administered in a short period of time (six to eight hours). Because of the site visit schedule and the limited descriptive (as opposed to evaluative) role of the case studies, interviewers had little opportunity to observe programs at the institutions or to talk to staff other than the specific DPQ respondents. However, when the interviews with study group members took place during the summer, many of the field interviewers visited the institutions to observe the prerelease and residential programs in which individuals had participated.

Gathering Data on the Study Group and their Families

Field Staff Selection and Training.   A total of 14 field staff members were hired by Abt Associates to conduct the interviews and gather the data. Two types of field staff were recruited: field interviewers, who were responsible for conducting the interviews with deinstitutionalized individuals and their families; and field supervisors, who, in addition to conducting interviews, were also responsible for making the initial contacts with study group members and their families, scheduling interviews at the sites, and supervising the work of the field interview teams.   Field staff members were recruited from universities, school systems, and programs and facilities serving mentally retarded persons; they included special education teachers, rehabilitation counselors, group home staff, psychologists, and staff from state institutions for the mentally retarded.

All field staff underwent four days of intensive training. During the initial training sessions, they were introduced to the project as a whole and to each of the data collection instruments. A training manual outlining all field procedures was provided to each staff member to be utilized on-site. In subsequent training sessions field staff were instructed in general interviewing practices and specific methods for administering each of the instruments to be used in the study. Item specifications were provided to clarify the intent of each   question in the instruments. Potential problems in the field were also discussed, and possible solutions suggested.

Role-playing techniques were utilized in the training sessions to give field staff practice in conducting and recording interviews. In addition, a house manager of a group residence for mentally retarded persons and a mentally retarded individual living independently in the community served as sample respondents. Each field staff member had an opportunity to interview these persons. In order further to orient the staff to the sensitive process of interviewing mentally retarded persons and their families, the Mohawks, a Massachusetts-based group of mentally retarded adults who conduct training and sensitivity session for professionals, met with the field staff to inform them about the problems of living in the community and being interviewed in studies such as the Abt project.

Field Effort. A field team was stationed at each of the nine sites to conduct interviews with members of the study group and their families. In most cases, the team consisted of one field supervisor and one field interviewer. In a few cases, however, the teams were larger because of the number of respondents at the site or because of the distances involved in travelling to respondents' homes. At one site, where only a small number of study group members were located, one field supervisor conducted all the interviews in that area.

The overall field effort was supervised and coordinated by an Abt Associates field coordinator. All field supervisors were required to report to the field coordinator daily while in the field to discuss the field team's work and any problems or questions.

Interview appointments for field staff were arranged before the actual site visit by each team's field supervisor. To minimize travel time, a field staff member would conduct interviews with all persons living in a particular town before travelling to another area in the site.

Study group members were given the choice of being interviewed in their homes, at the institution, at the interviewer's hotel, or at any other location requested. Almost all of the interviews were conducted at the residences or at the institution (mostly in the case of those who had returned). Some individuals were interviewed at their place of work to avoid interrupting their work schedules.

The interviews were conducted during July, August, September, and October of 1975. On the average, field staff members conducted two family interviews and two resident interviews a day, although this varied depending on the location and type of setting involved. For example, at a group home, the field staff member might conduct separate interviews with the house manager and three residents in one day. This was possible because all three residents were in one setting and the house manager served as the respondent for each of them. However, if the study group member was living with his or her natural family in an outlying rural setting, it was sometimes possible to conduct only one family and one resident interview in a day.

Generally, a family interview took two to three hours. The Resident Questionnaire was completed in about 45 minutes. The interview with a mentally retarded person living independently combined these two questionnaires and took about three hours. The interview with the contact person for the individual living independently usually took one to one and a half hours.

After the field effort was completed, a half-day debriefing meeting was conducted at Abt Associates. At this meeting, team members' overall impressions of the field effort were discussed, as well as specific observations; criticisms, and suggestions regarding particular items in each of the questionnaires.

In general, the field staff felt that they were well received at the sites. The study group members, their families, and any staff who participated (at the request of individuals or families) were most cooperative. Although the interview sessions were long, respondents seemed eager to provide field staff with the necessary information. Often, they used the interview as an opportunity to vent their feelings and give "their side of the story."

The field procedures used in this study imposed three major limitations on the data. First, the data were collected during the summer months and early fall. This particular period of time was selected to meet study deadlines and to attract competent interviewers who might not be available at another time (e.g., special education teachers and graduate students). However, certain individuals may have been unable to participate in the study because of conflicts in schedules, such as vacations. Every attempt was made to schedule appointments at the respondents' convenience. In fact, in many cases, interviewers returned to certain areas to interview those persons who were not interviewed initially because they were unavailable. However, a small number of persons were not included in the study because their schedules could not be accommodated.

Second, in collecting the data, no attempt was made to verify the accuracy of the information provided by the respondents; perceptions were taken at face value. In cases where two respondents in an interview provided discrepant information, they were both contacted to "adjust" the discrepancies. If the two parties insisted that their information was accurate, both responses were recorded.

Finally, it was difficult to control for the fact that some respondents may have answered questions too positively; that is, they may have overstated how well they were doing in the community in order to please the interviewer or out of fear that information about their adjustment would be given to the institution. Every effort was made to reassure respondents about the confidentiality of the information and the importance of responding as honestly as possible. However, some respondents may still have felt compelled, for whatever reason, to respond less than accurately.

DATA ANALYSIS AND REPORTING

The information collected and the subsequent reports issued are listed in Figure A.1. The present book was undertaken to supplement these reports by aggregating the salient findings and reporting them in a more descriptive manner appropriate to a wide spectrum of readers.

Appendix B
Additional Data On Individual Characteristics and Institutional Experiences

TABLE B.1
NUMBER OF ADDITIONAL DISABILITIES
BY AGE

Number	Children		Adults		Total	
	N(83)	%	N(357)	%	N(440)	%
0	22	27	158	44	180	41
1	23	28	113	32	136	31
2	18	22	54	15	72	16
3	9	11	27	8	36	8
4	6	7	4	1	10	2
5	4	5	1	<1	5	1
6	1	1	0	0	1	<1

TABLE B.2
NUMBER OF ADDITIONAL DISABILITIES BY
LEVEL OF RETARDATION

	Level of Retardation							
Number	Mild		Moderate		Severe		Total	
	N	%	N	%	N	%	N	%
0	78	46	65	47	31	29	180	41
1	49	29	45	33	32	30	136	31
2	29	17	12	9	25	24	72	16
3	13	8	12	9	9	9	36	8
4	2	1	3	2	4	4	10	2
5	0		0		4	4	5	1
6	0		0		1	1	1	<1

TABLE B.3
TYPE OF DAY PLACEMENT BY AGE

Type	Children N(43)	%	Adults N(272)	%	Total N(315)	%
Community and institutions	36	84	197	72	233	74
Community only	7	16	75	28	82	26

TABLE B.4
TYPE OF DAY PLACEMENT BY LEVEL OF RETARDATION

	Level of Retardation							
Type	Mild N(145)	%	Moderate N(99)	%	Severe N(55)	%	Total N(299)	%
Community and institution	101	70	77	78	46	84	224	75
Community only	44	30	22	22	9	16	75	25

TABLE B.5
SATISFACTION WITH PRERELEASE PLACEMENT BY AGE

Satisfaction	Children N(76)	%	Adults N(305)	%	Total N(381)	%
Satisfied	50	66	206	68	256	67
Dissatisfied	26	34	99	32	125	33

TABLE B.6
SATISFACTION WITH PRERELEASE PLACEMENT
BY LEVEL OF RETARDATION

	Level of Retardation							
Satisfaction	Mild N(150)	%	Moderate N(118)	%	Severe N(90)	%	Total N(358)	%
Satisfied	106	71	81	69	52	58	239	67
Dissatisfied	44	29	37	31	38	42	119	33

TABLE B.7
INSTITUTIONAL TRAINING

Area of Training	Received, Adequate		Received, Inadequate		Needed, Did Not Get		Not Ready		Did Not Get		Total
	N	%	N	%	N	%	N	%	N	%	
Personal Maintenance											
Eating	147	37	54	14	15	4	2	1	181	45	399
Using toilet	126	32	32	8	8	2	7	2	225	57	398
Dressing	155	40	30	8	6	2	8	2	185	48	384
Cleanliness	145	38	92	24	14	4	9	2	121	32	381
Grooming	155	40	93	24	26	7	12	3	99	26	385
Sensory Development											
Motor	115	29	40	10	18	5	8	2	209	54	390
Hearing and vision	108	27	23	6	16	4	4	1	245	62	396
Speech and language	112	30	89	24	54	15	6	2	110	30	371
Education and employment											
Preacademic	132	37	53	15	37	10	21	6	119	33	362
Numbers and telling time	104	28	99	27	55	15	60	16	52	14	370
Reading and writing	82	22	107	29	63	17	91	24	30	8	373
Prevocational	157	42	79	21	46	12	83	22	12	3	377
Vocational	114	29	70	18	74	19	126	33	4	1	388
Domestic Living											
Housekeeping	195	52	76	20	25	7	33	9	44	12	373
Meals preparation	109	28	48	12	135	35	69	18	26	7	387
Shopping	72	18	67	17	120	30	108	27	29	7	396
Money management	63	15	80	20	128	31	115	28	22	5	408
Use of Community Resources											
Travel and mobility	78	19	50	12	147	37	98	24	39	9	412
Using the telephone	81	21	31	8	122	31	103	26	54	14	391
Coping with emergencies	54	14	34	9	141	37	139	36	17	4	385
Using community agencies	31	8	17	4	150	37	201	50	7	2	406
Behavior Management											
Interpersonal relationships	145	39	130	35	58	16	21	6	15	4	369
Behavior control	145	39	138	37	45	12	12	3	33	9	373
Social and recreational activities	234	67	73	21	23	7	11	3	10	3	351

Appendix C
Additional Data On Residences

TABLE C.1
TYPES OF DWELLINGS BY TYPE OF SETTING

Types of Dwellings	Natural Home		Foster Home		Group Home		Semi-Independent		Independent		Total	
	N(54)	%	N(50)	%	N(188)	%	N(40)	%	N(46)	%(103)	N(37)	%
Single family	46	84	42	84	122	65	9	22	8	17	227	60
2 to 4 families	1	4	1	2	11	6	14	35	12	26	39	10
5 or more families	2	4	—	—	8	4	8	20	11	26	30	8
Rooming house	—	—	—	—	—	—	1	2	5	12	6	2
Mobile home	2	4	1	2	—	—	—	—	—	—	3	1
Other	3	6	6	12	47	25	8	21	10	22	73	19

TABLE C.2
INTERIOR CONDITION OF RESIDENCES BY TYPE OF SETTING

Condition of Interior	Natural Home		Foster Home		Group Home		Semi-Independent		Independent		Total	
	N(53)	%	N(50)	%	N(188)	%	N(40)	%	N(45)	%	N(376)	%
Excellent condition (in excellent repair, well painted)	31	58	31	62	101	54	21	53	16	36	200	53
Moderate condition (moderately well kept up, but in need of some repairs)	12	23	11	22	61	32	13	32	11	24	108	29
Poor condition (in poor repair, paint peeling off walls, falling apart)	7	13	3	6	0	0	0	0	10	22	20	5
Not ascertainable (interview held outside of residence)	3	6	5	10	26	14	6	15	8	18	48	13

TABLE C.3
CLEANLINESS OF RESIDENCES BY TYPE OF SETTING

Cleanliness of Home	Natural Home		Foster Home		Group Home		Semi- Independent		Independent		Total	
	N(51)	%	N(44)	%	N(163)	%	N(34)	%	N(36)	%	N(328)	%
Very clean	34	67	28	64	117	72	19	56	16	44	214	65
Reasonably clean	7	14	10	23	36	22	14	41	11	31	78	24
Somewhat dirty	4	87	6	14	10	6	1	3	4	11	25	8
Extremely dirty	6	12	—	—	—	—	—	—	5	14	11	3

TABLE C.4
HOMELIKE CHARACTERISTICS OF RESIDENCES BY TYPE OF SETTING

Scale of Homelike Characteristics	Natural Home N(53)	%	Foster Home N(50)	%	Group Home N(188)	%	Semi-Independent N(40)	%	Independent N(44)	%	Total N(315)	%
High (Residence is very homelike, e.g., comfortable furnishings personal possessions visible, homelike rhythms to daily activities	49	92	44	88	149	79	28	70	32	73	302	81
Moderate (residence has some homelike aspects but also has some institutional touches, e.g., few pictures or personal possessions visible)	1	2	1	2	12	6	6	15	3	7	23	6
Low (residence is very institutional, e.g., sign on front door, pay telephone, no personal possessions visible)	—	—	—	—	1	1	—	—	—	—	1	<1
Not Ascertainable (interview was held outside of residence)	3	6	5	10	26	14	6	15	9	20	49	13

TABLE C.5
DISTANCE OF RESIDENCES FROM SHOPPING AREA BY TYPE OF SETTING

Distance From Shopping Area	Natural Home		Foster Home		Group Home		Semi-Independent		Independent		Total	
	N(55)	%	N(51)	%	N(186)	%	N(40)	%	N(46)	%	N(378)	%
Less than one-half mile	22	40	26	51	138	74	31	77	40	87	257	68
One-half to one mile	11	20	10	20	19	10	6	15	4	9	50	13
More than one mile	22	40	15	29	29	16	3	7	2	4	71	19

TABLE C.6

DISTANCE OF RESIDENCES FROM PUBLIC TRANSPORTATION BY TYPE OF SETTING

Distance from Bus, Trolley, or Subway	Natural Home		Foster Home		Group Home		Semi-Independent		Independent		Total	
	N(55)	%	N(51)	%	N(186)	%	N(40)	%	N(46)	%	N(378)	%
Less than one-half mile	22	40	17	33	108	58	23	57	27	59	197	52
One-half to one mile	4	7	9	18	2	1	2	5	5	11	22	6
More than one mile	5	9	6	12	9	5	1	2	1	2	22	6
No public transportation available	24	44	19	37	67	36	14	35	13	28	137	36

TABLE C.7
FREQUENCY OF PUBLIC TRANSPORTATION
BY TYPE OF RESIDENTIAL SETTING

How Often Bus or Subway Runs	Natural Home N(30)	%	Foster Home N(28)	%	Group Home N(46)	%	Semi-Independent N(25)	%	Independent N(31)	%	Total N(230)	%
At least once every half-hour	10	33	11	39	44	38	13	52	9	29	87	38
About once every hour	9	30	6	22	43	37	11	44	12	39	81	35
Two to six times a day	11	37	11	39	29	25	1	4	10	32	62	27

TABLE C.8
SATISFACTION WITH RESIDENCE BY AGE

Likes/Dislikes	Children		Adults		Total	
	N(59)	%	N(327)	%	N(386)	%
Likes home	55	93	294	90	349	90
Dislikes home	4	7	33	10	37	10

TABLE C.9
SATISFACTION WITH RESIDENCE BY LEVEL OF RETARDATION

	Level of Retardation					
Likes/Dislikes	Mild		Moderate		Severe	
	N(165)	%	N(123)	%	N(74)	%
Likes home	146	88.5	108	88	71	96
Dislikes home	19	11.5	15	12	3	4

TABLE C.10
FAMILY PERCEPTIONS OF ADJUSTMENT TO HOUSE
AND RESIDENTS BY AGE

	Adjustment to House					
Adjustment Rating	Children		Adults		Total	
	N(84)	%	N(348)	%	N(432)	%
Good	66	79	251	72	317	73
Fair	14	17	71	20	85	20
Poor	4	5	26	8	30	7

	Adjustment to Other Residents					
Adjustment Rating	Children		Adults		Total	
	N(74)	%	N(338)	%	N(417)	%
Good	54	68	220	65	274	66
Fair	15	19	84	25	99	24
Poor	10	13	34	10	44	10

TABLE C.11
RESIDENT'S PERCEPTIONS OF ADJUSTMENT TO
HOUSE AND RESIDENTS BY AGE

| Adjustment | Adjustment to the House | | | | | |
| | Children | | Adults | | Total | |
Rating	N(55)	%	N(263)	%	N(378)	
Good	47	86	185	70	232	
Fair	5	9	56	21	61	
Poor	3	5	22	9	25	

| Adjustment | Adjustment to Other Residents | | | | | |
| | Children | | Adults | | Total | |
Rating	N(51)	%	N(253)	%	N(304)	
Good	32	63	160	63	912	
Fair	12	23	73	29	85	
Poor	7	14	20	8	27	

TABLE C.12
RESIDENT'S PERCEPTIONS OF ADJUSTMENT TO HOUSE AND
RESIDENTS BY LEVEL OF RETARDATION

| Adjustment | Adjustment to the House | | | | | | | |
| | Mild | | Moderate | | Severe | | Total | |
Rating	N(131)	%	N(103)	%	N(66)	%	N(300)	
Good	84	64	77	74	54	82	215	
Fair	36	28	13	13	8	12	57	
Poor	11	8	13	13	4	6	30	

| Adjustment | Adjustment to Other Residents | | | | | | | |
| | Mild | | Moderate | | Severe | | Total | |
Rating	N(124)	%	N(102)	%	N(63)	%	N(289)	
Good	72	58	68	67	40	63	180	
Fair	38	31	25	24	18	29	81	
Poor	14	11	9	9	5	8	28	

TABLE C.13
FAMILY PERCEPTIONS OF ADJUSTMENT OF HOUSE
AND RESIDENTS BY LEVEL OF RETARDATION

			Adjustment to House				
Adjustment	Mild		Moderate		Severe		Total
Rating	N(164)	%	N(132)	%	N(104)	%	N(400)
Good	115	70	94	71	83	80	292
Fair	36	22	27	21	15	14	78
Poor	13	8	11	8	6	6	30
			Adjustment to Other Residents				
Adjustment	Mild		Moderate		Severe		Total
Rating	N(157)	%	N(133)	%	N(100)	%	N(390)
Good	96	61	81	61	72	72	249
Fair	44	28	36	27	19	19	99
Poor	17	11	16	12	9	9	32

Appendix D
Additional Data On
Leisure And Social Activities

TABLE D.1
PARTICIPATION IN LEISURE TIME ACTIVITIES
BY LEVEL OF RETARDATION

Type of Activity	Did Participate		Did Not Participate		Total
	N	%	N	%	N
Watching TV, Listening to Radio					
Mild	171	100	—	—	171
Moderate	134	99	2	1	136
Severe	100	95	5	5	105
Shopping or Errands					
Mild	163	95	8	5	171
Moderate	120	89	15	11	135
Severe	68	66	35	34	103
Movies					
Mild	147	87	23	13	170
Moderate	118	87	17	13	135
Severe	75	71	30	29	105
Vacations					
Mild	129	77	39	23	168
Moderate	114	84	21	16	135
Severe	74	70	31	30	105
Parties					
Mild	122	71	49	29	171
Moderate	106	79	28	21	134
Severe	79	75	26	25	
Religious Activities					
Mild	125	75	42	25	167
Moderate	95	72	37	28	132
Severe	71	68	33	32	104
Visit Friends					
Mild	127	74	44	26	171
Moderate	93	69	41	31	134
Severe	69	67	34	33	103
Play Sports					
Mild	107	64	61	36	168
Moderate	103	76	32	24	135
Severe	77	74	27	26	104
Hobbies					
Mild	120	71	48	29	168
Moderate	80	60	54	40	134
Severe	52	50	52	50	104
Attend Sports Events					
Mild	93	56	74	44	167
Moderate	81	60	55	40	136
Severe	61	59	43	41	104
Go on Dates[a]					
Mild	65	40	97	60	162
Moderate	36	28	91	72	127
Severe	86	82	19	18	105
Attend Club Meetings					
Mild	34	20	135	80	169
Moderate	28	21	108	79	136
Severe	14	13	91	87	105

[a] Asked only about individuals over age 12.

TABLE D.2
PARTICIPATION IN LEISURE ACTIVITIES BY AGE

Activity	Did Participate		Did Not Participate		Total
	N	%	N	%	N
Watching TV, Listening to Radio					
Children	81	95	4	5	85
Adults	351	99	4	1	355
Shopping or Errands					
Children	63	76	20	24	83
Adults	312	88	43	12	355
Movies					
Children	63	74	22	26	85
Adults	307	87	48	14	355
Vacations					
Children	72	85	13	15	85
Adults	288	81	67	19	355
Parties					
Children	55	65	30	35	85
Adults	276	78	80	22	355
Religious Activities					
Children	58	68	27	32	85
Adults	253	72	97	28	350
Visit Friends					
Children	56	67	28	33	84
Adults	262	74	93	26	355
Play Sports					
Children	65	76	20	24	85
Adults	245	70	109	31	354
Hobbies					
Children	43	51	42	49	85
Adults	230	65	122	35	352
Attend Sports Events					
Children	45	53	40	47	85
Adults	211	60	143	40	354
Go on Dates[a]					
Children	7	13	46	87	53
Adults	105	30	248	70	353
Attend Club Meetings					
Children	9	11	76	89	85
Adults	78	22	277	78	355

[a] Asked only about individuals over 12 years old.

TABLE D.3
ACTIVITIES ALLOWED/NOT ALLOWED
BY AGE

Activity	Did Participate		Did Not Participate		Total
	N	%	N	%	N
Dinner Guests					
Children	64	96	3	4	67
Adults	275	95	14	5	289
Overnight Guests					
Children	47	72	18	28	65
Adults	181	64	100	36	281
Come and Go at Will					
Children	4	6	64	94	68
Adults	106	36	187	64	293
Decide When to Go to Sleep					
Children	34	47	39	53	73
Adults	243	79	63	21	306
Wear Clothing of Own Choice or Style					
Children	54	77	16	23	70
Adults	287	94	20	6	307
Decide What Clothes to Purchase					
Children	44	64	25	36	69
Adults	259	85	45	15	304
Wear Hair in Own Choice of Style					
Children	45	62	28	38	73
Adults	272	89	35	11	307
Decide How to Spend Own Money					
Children	48	69	22	31	70
Adults	252	82	55	18	307
Go on Dates Outside of Home[a]					
Children	31	45	38	55	69
Adults	231	76	74	24	305
Drink Alcoholic Beverages in Home					
Children	28	42	39	58	67
Adults	132	43	177	57	309
Decide When to Make Appointment					
Children	27	40	40	60	67
Adults	182	60	119	40	301

[a] Asked only about individuals over age 12.

TABLE D.4
ACTIVITIES ALLOWED/NOT ALLOWED
BY LEVEL OF RETARDATION

Activity	Allowed		Not Allowed		Total
	N	%	N	%	N
Dinner Guests					
Mild	106	92	9	8	115
Moderate	127	96	5	4	132
Severe	77	94	5	6	82
Overnight Guests					
Mild	74	66	39	34	113
Moderate	87	67	42	33	129
Severe	46	60	31	40	77
Come and Go at Will					
Mild	43	36	77	64	120
Moderate	44	33	91	68	135
Severe	17	20	68	80	85
Decide When to Go to Sleep					
Mild	96	77	28	23	124
Moderate	99	72	38	28	137
Severe	58	64	33	36	91
Wear Clothing of Own Choice and Style					
Mild	113	90	12	10	125
Moderate	130	95	7	5	137
Severe	74	84	14	16	88
Decide What Clothes to Purchase					
Mild	104	85	19	15	123
Moderate	123	90	14	10	137
Severe	57	65	31	35	88
Wear Hair in Own Choice of Style					
Mild	110	88	15	12	125
Moderate	123	90	14	10	137
Severe	65	71	27	29	92
Decide How to Spend Own Money					
Mild	104	83	21	17	125
Moderate	119	87	18	13	137
Severe	54	61	34	39	88
Go on Dates Outside of Home[a]					
Mild	87	70	27	30	114
Moderate	113	83	24	17	137
Severe	44	51	43	49	87
Drink Alcoholic Beverages in the Home[b]					
Mild	59	47	66	53	125
Moderate	62	46	74	54	136
Severe	28	31	62	69	90
Decide When to Make Appointments					
Mild	73	59	51	41	124
Moderate	87	64	49	36	136
Severe	35	41	50	59	85

[a] Asked only about individuals over age 12.

[b] Asked only about individuals over age 18 or the age of majority in the state.

TABLE D.5
FAMILY RATINGS OF COMPETENCE IN MANAGING
ROMANTIC RELATIONSHIPS BY LEVEL OF RETARDATION

| Managed | Level of Retardation | | | | | |
| | Mild | | Moderate | | Severe | |
Relationship	N	%	N	%	N	%
Very well	51	49	32	55	12	46
All right	28	27	16	28	11	42
Not very well	25	24	10	17	3	12

TABLE D.6
FAMILY RATINGS OF COMPETENCE IN MANAGING
ROMANTIC RELATIONSHIPS BY AGE

| Managed Relationship | Children | | Adults | |
	N	%	N	%
Very well	6	33	93	51
All right	5	28	54	30
Not very well	7	39	35	19

TABLE D.7
FAMILY PERCEPTIONS OF PROBLEMS WITH
SOCIAL RELATIONSHIPS BY LEVEL OF RETARDATION

| Extent of Problem | Level of Retardation | | | | | |
| | Mild | | Moderate | | Severe | |
	N	%	N	%	N	%
Big problem	27	16	22	16	9	9
Somewhat of a problem	44	27	36	27	20	20
Not a problem	95	57	77	57	73	71

TABLE D.8
FAMILY PERCEPTIONS OF PROBLEMS WITH
LONELINESS BY LEVEL OF RETARDATION

Extent of Problem	Level of Retardation					
	Mild		Moderate		Severe	
	N	%	N	%	N	%
Big problem	26	16	15	11	5	5
Somewhat of a problem	50	30	38	28	17	17
Not a problem	91	54	84	61	79	78

Appendix E
Additional Data On Services

TABLE E.1
SOURCES OF PERSONAL SUPPORT OR FOLLOW-UP
BY LEVEL OF RETARDATION

Source	Level of Retardation	Received or Has		Has Not Received/ Does Not Have	
		N	%	N	%
Institutional follow-up	Mild	103	61	65	39
	Moderate	83	61	52	39
	Severe	62	60	41	40
Community case manager	Mild	159	97	5	3
	Moderate	130	96	5	4
	Severe	101	97	3	3
Nonprofessional individual (relative or friend)	Mild	134	80	34	20
	Moderate	103	77	31	23
	Severe	64	62	39	38

TABLE E.2
SOURCES OF PERSONAL SUPPORT OR FOLLOW-UP
BY AGE

Source	Age	Received or Has		Has Not Received/ Does Not Have	
		N	%	N	%
Institutional follow-up	Children	53	63	31	37
	Adults	208	59	146	41
Community case manager	Children	81	98	2	2
	Adults	342	97	10	3
Nonprofessional individual (relative or friend)	Children	44	54	38	46
	Adults	278	78	77	22

TABLE E.3

UTILIZATION OF AND NEED FOR SERVICES BY AGE LEVEL

Type of Service	Age	Used		Needed, Not Used		Not Needed, Not Used		Total	
		N	%	N	%	N	%	N	%
Medical and Health Care									
Medical services	Children	79	93	2	2	4	5	85	100
	Adults	131	84	2	1	23	15	156	100
Dental services	Children	63	72	17	19	8	9	88	100
	Adults	275	77	20	6	61	17	356	100
Physical therapy	Children	17	20	9	11	59	69	85	100
	Adults	34	10	18	5	306	85	358	100
Speech therapy	Children	34	40	20	24	31	36	85	100
	Adults	99	28	51	14	207	58	357	100
Social and Recreational Services									
Recreational therapy	Children	69	82	8	9	8	9	85	100
	Adults	291	81	29	8	38	11	358	100
Social and psychological services	Children	36	43	9	11	39	46	84	100
	Adults	219	62	25	7	112	31	356	100
Camp programs	Children	41	54	10	13	25	33	76	100
	Adults	123	40	40	13	144	47	307	100
Occupational therapy	Children	27	31	11	13	48	56	86	100
	Adults	113	32	30	8	216	60	359	100
Employment Services									
Employment placement and support services	Children	13	16	5	6	64	78	82	100
	Adults	210	59	19	5	126	36	355	100
Housing and Legal Services									
Housing assistance	Children	8	9	1	1	76	90	85	100
	Adults	95	27	9	3	252	70	356	100
Legal assistance	Children	8	10	3	4	72	86	83	100
	Adults	35	10	7	2	315	88	357	100

TABLE E.4
PROVIDERS OF SERVICES USED BY AGE LEVEL

Type of Service	Age	Institution		Residence		Day/Work Program		Community Agency		Private Providers		Total	
		N	%	N	%	N	%	N	%	N	%	N	%
Medical and Health Care													
Medical services	Children	23	24	8	8	—	—	35	36	31	32	97	100
	Adults	69	18	28	7	7	2	151	38	135	35	390	100
Dental services	Children	26	36	7	10	3	4	17	24	19	26	72	100
	Adults	68	22	13	4	2	1	112	35	119	38	314	100
Physical therapy	Children	5	17	7	23	9	30	8	27	1	3	30	100
	Adults	9	19	5	10	9	19	24	50	1	2	48	100
Speech therapy	Children	3	7	4	10	23	55	11	26	1	2	42	100
	Adults	14	10	20	14	37	27	62	45	5	4	138	100
Social and Recreational Services													
Recreational therapy	Children	3	3	41	35	33	28	39	34	—	—	116	100
	Adults	19	4	170	38	95	21	167	37	1	1	452	100
Social and psychological therapy	Children	11	26	5	12	7	16	20	47	—	—	43	100
	Adults	40	14	50	17	48	16	142	49	12	4	292	100
Camp programs	Children	6	13	9	20	6	13	24	54	—	—	45	100
	Adults	11	7	17	11	21	13	106	68	1	1	156	100
Occupational therapy	Children	1	3	9	28	15	47	7	22	—	—	32	100
	Adults	5	4	22	17	72	57	25	20	2	2	126	100
Employment Services													
Employment placement and support services	Children	2	11	4	22	9	50	3	17	—	—	18	100
	Adults	32	12	39	15	106	41	80	31	3	1	260	100
Housing and Legal Services													
Housing assistance	Children	—	—	2	25	—	—	6	75	—	—	8	100
	Adults	7	7	36	34	4	4	57	54	1	1	105	100
Legal assistance	Children	—	—	3	30	—	—	7	70	—	—	10	100
	Adults	3	7	11	26	6	14	14	33	8	20	42	100

TABLE E.5
UTILIZATION OF AND NEED FOR SERVICES BY LEVEL OF RETARDATION

Type of Service	Level of Retardation	Used N	Used %	Needed, Not Used N	Needed, Not Used %	Not Needed, Not Used N	Not Needed, Not Used %	Total N	Total %
Medical and Health Care									
Medical services	Mild	160	94	2	1	9	5	171	100
	Moderate	124	93	1	1	9	6	134	100
	Severe	98	94	2	2	4	4	104	100
Dental services	Mild	125	72	18	10	30	18	173	100
	Moderate	112	84	5	3	17	13	134	100
	Severe	74	71	13	12	18	17	105	100
Physical therapy	Mild	14	8	8	5	148	87	170	100
	Moderate	9	7	4	3	123	90	136	100
	Severe	19	18	14	13	72	69	105	100
Speech therapy	Mild	34	20	14	8	122	72	170	100
	Moderate	36	28	23	18	71	54	130	100
	Severe	48	46	31	30	26	24	105	100
Social and Recreational Services									
Recreational therapy	Mild	128	75	18	11	24	14	170	100
	Moderate	113	83	9	7	14	10	136	100
	Severe	92	88	9	9	4	3	105	100
Social and psycho-logical therapy	Mild	103	61	21	13	44	26	168	100
	Moderate	83	61	7	5	46	34	136	100
	Severe	52	50	3	3	49	47	104	100
Camp programs	Mild	51	34	24	16	76	50	151	100
	Moderate	48	45	11	10	48	45	107	100
	Severe	50	53	12	13	32	34	94	100
Occupational therapy	Mild	54	31	15	9	105	60	174	100
	Moderate	38	28	14	10	84	62	136	100
	Severe	40	38	10	10	54	52	104	100
Employment Services									
Employment place-ment and support services	Mild	112	66	12	7	45	27	169	100
	Moderate	65	49	8	6	61	45	134	100
	Severe	32	31	4	4	67	65	103	100
Housing and Legal Services									
Housing assistance	Mild	51	30	6	4	113	66	170	100
	Moderate	29	22	3	2	102	76	134	100
	Severe	16	15	1	1	88	84	105	100
Legal assistance	Mild	17	10	4	2	148	88	169	100
	Moderate	12	9	2	1	121	90	135	100
	Severe	10	10	2	2	92	88	104	100

TABLE E.6
UTILIZATION OF AND NEED FOR SUPPORT SERVICES FOR FAMILIES
OF THE RETARDED BY AGE LEVEL

Type of Service	Age	Used		Needed, Not Received		Not Needed, Not Received		Total	
		N	%	N	%	N	%	N	%
Support and/or training prior to individual's release	Children	19	23	25	30	39	47	83	100
	Adults	104	34	76	25	127	41	307	100
General counseling	Children	37	44	14	17	32	39	83	100
	Adults	178	58	31	10	97	32	306	100
Consultation for handling specific problem	Children	58	70	9	11	16	19	83	100
	Adults	244	79	19	6	47	15	310	100
Temporary relief from responsibilities	Children	44	53	11	13	28	34	83	100
	Adults	170	64	23	8	74	28	267	100
Parent or professional associations	Children	39	48	16	19	27	33	82	100
	Adults	126	41	47	15	135	44	308	100

TABLE E.7

UTILIZATION OF AND NEED FOR SUPPORT SERVICES
FOR FAMILIES OF THE RETARDED BY LEVEL OF RETARDATION

Type of Service	Level of Retardation	Used		Needed, Not Received		Not Needed, Not Received		Total	
		N	%	N	%	N	%	N	%
Support and/or training prior to individual's release	Mild	51	38	27	20	57	42	135	100
	Moderate	46	38	28	23	48	39	122	100
	Severe	24	23	28	27	53	50	105	100
General counseling	Mild	77	58	11	8	46	34	134	100
	Moderate	75	61	11	9	37	30	123	100
	Severe	57	54	9	9	39	37	105	100
Consultation for handling specific problems	Mild	105	78	8	6	22	16	135	100
	Moderate	95	77	6	5	23	18	124	100
	Severe	81	76	9	9	16	15	106	100
Temporary relief from responsibilities	Mild	73	63	7	6	36	31	116	100
	Moderate	74	67	10	9	27	24	111	100
	Severe	52	53	14	14	33	33	99	100
Parent or professional associations	Mild	44	33	18	13	73	54	135	100
	Moderate	64	53	17	14	40	33	121	100
	Severe	42	40	21	20	43	40	106	100

Appendix F
Additional Data On Training

TABLE F.1

UTILIZATION OF AND NEED FOR TRAINING BY AGE LEVEL

Type of Training	Age	Received		Needed, Not Received		Not Needed, Not Received				Total	
						Already Had Skill		Not Ready for Skill			
		N	%	N	%	N	%	N	%	N	%
Personal Maintenance											
Eating	Children	59	72	3	4	18	22	2	2	82	100
	Adults	150	53	1	1	131	46	—		282	100
Using the toilet	Children	41	51	2	3	33	41	4	5	80	100
	Adults	25	9	1	1	246	89	3	1	275	100
Dressing	Children	37	45	2	3	38	46	5	6	82	100
	Adults	64	23	2	1	213	76	—		279	100
Cleanliness	Children	66	80	2	3	10	12	4	5	82	100
	Adults	173	60	1	1	114	39	1	1	289	100
Grooming	Children	58	70	1	1	15	18	9	11	83	100
	Adults	186	64	1	1	102	35	—		289	100
Sensory Development											
Motor	Children	38	46	7	8	37	44	2	2	84	100
	Adults	93	28	11	3	232	68	3	1	339	100
Hearing and vision	Children	29	35	2	2	51	62	1	1	83	100
	Adults	48	14	6	2	279	84	1	1	334	100
Speech and language	Children	61	77	6	8	11	14	1	1	79	100
	Adults	154	46	36	11	142	42	4	1	336	100
Education and Employment											
Preacademic	Children	59	73	1	1	17	21	4	5	81	100
	Adults	128	39	11	3	185	56	5	2	329	100
Numbers and telling time	Children	59	74	2	2	3	4	16	20	80	100
	Adults	188	56	29	9	91	27	27	8	335	100
Reading and writing	Children	58	72	2	2	1	1	20	25	81	100
	Adults	192	56	37	11	61	18	51	15	341	100
Prevocational	Children	35	44	3	4	1	1	41	51	80	100
	Adults	236	69	12	3	76	22	21	6	345	100
Vocational	Children	17	21	6	8	1	1	57	70	81	100
	Adults	198	58	27	8	43	13	74	21	342	100

TABLE F.1 (CONTINUED)

Type of Training	Age	Received		Needed, Not Received		Not Needed, Not Received				Total	
---	---	---	---	---	---	Already Had Skill		Not Ready for Skill			
		N	%	N	%	N	%	N	%	N	%
Domestic Living											
Housekeeping	Children	56	69	5	6	7	9	13	16	81	100
	Adults	234	69	6	2	95	28	4	1	339	100
Meal preparation	Children	61	73	—		4	5	19	23	84	100
	Adults	256	73	16	4	55	16	24	7	351	100
Shopping	Children	40	47	2	2	4	5	39	46	85	100
	Adults	228	66	16	5	64	18	40	11	348	100
Money management	Children	37	43	7	8	1	1	41	48	86	100
	Adults	230	65	28	8	36	10	59	17	353	100
Use of Community Resources											
Travel and mobility	Children	30	35	7	8	9	10	40	47	86	100
	Adults	190	54	20	6	96	27	44	13	350	100
Using the telephone	Children	34	40	2	2	11	13	39	45	86	100
	Adults	140	42	26	8	113	33	58	17	337	100
Coping with emergencies	Children	24	29	10	11	5	6	45	54	84	100
	Adults	166	48	40	11	66	19	76	22	348	100
Using community agencies	Children	5	6	8	9	3	4	67	81	83	100
	Adults	91	27	34	10	52	15	166	48	343	100
Behavior Management											
Interpersonal relation-ships	Children	68	79	6	7	4	5	8	9	86	100
	Adults	270	77	15	4	59	17	7	2	351	100
Behavior control	Children	72	85	2	2	6	7	5	6	85	100
	Adults	241	69	10	3	91	26	5	2	347	100
Social and recreational activities	Children	77	92			4	5	3	2	84	100
	Adults	268	77	18	5	57	16	6	2	349	100

TABLE F.2
UTILIZATION OF AND NEED FOR TRAINING BY LEVEL OF RETARDATION

Type of Training	Level of Retardation	Received		Needed, Not Received		Not Needed, Not Received				Total	
						Already Had Skill		Not Ready for Skill			
		N	%	N	%	N	%	N	%	N	%
Personal Maintenance											
Eating	Mild	57	46	1	1	65	53	—	0	123	100
	Moderate	56	50	—	0	56	50	—	—	112	100
	Severe	78	76	3	3	19	19	2	2	102	100
Using the toilet	Mild	12	10	—	0	111	90	—	0	123	100
	Moderate	11	10	2	2	95	88	—	0	108	100
	Severe	32	33	1	1	59	61	5	5	97	100
Dressing	Mild	14	11	—	0	110	89	—	0	124	100
	Moderate	29	26	—	0	82	74	—	0	111	100
	Severe	45	46	4	4	46	46	4	4	99	100
Cleanliness	Mild	65	51	1	1	61	48	—	0	127	100
	Moderate	81	70	—	0	35	30	—	0	116	100
	Severe	76	75	1	1	21	21	3	3	101	100
Grooming	Mild	68	53	1	1	58	45	1	1	128	100
	Moderate	86	74	1	1	29	25	—	0	117	100
	Severe	73	72	1	1	20	20	7	7	101	100
Sensory Development											
Motor	Mild	29	18	4	3	126	78	1	1	160	100
	Moderate	37	29	4	3	87	68	—	0	128	100
	Severe	48	47	8	8	46	44	1	1	103	100
Hearing and vision	Mild	17	11	—	0	139	88	1	1	157	100
	Moderate	19	15	5	4	104	81	—	0	128	100
	Severe	31	31	2	2	67	66	1	1	101	100
Speech and language	Mild	65	41	9	5	83	53	1	1	158	100
	Moderate	58	46	12	10	53	42	2	2	125	100
	Severe	75	75	15	15	8	8	2	2	100	100
Education and Employment											
Preacademic	Mild	42	27	2	1	112	71	1	1	157	100
	Moderate	52	42	5	4	64	52	2	2	123	100
	Severe	75	77	4	4	14	14	5	5	98	100
Numbers and telling time	Mild	79	50	10	6	69	43	1	1	159	100
	Moderate	88	70	12	10	17	13	9	7	126	100
	Severe	62	64	5	5	4	4	26	27	97	100
Reading and writing	Mild	90	55	19	12	47	29	8	4	164	100
	Moderate	86	68	12	10	10	8	17	14	125	100
	Severe	55	55	6	6	4	4	35	35	100	100
Prevocational	Mild	105	65	6	4	45	27	6	4	162	100
	Moderate	83	64	3	2	25	19	20	15	131	100
	Severe	67	68	3	3	1	1	28	28	99	100
Vocational	Mild	100	62	16	10	21	13	24	15	161	100
	Moderate	56	44	11	9	21	16	40	31	128	100
	Severe	41	41	6	6	1	1	53	52	101	100

TABLE F.2 (CONTINUED)

Type of Training	Level of Retardation	Received N	Received %	Needed, Not Received N	Needed, Not Received %	Not Needed, Not Received — Already Had Skill N	Already Had Skill %	Not Ready for Skill N	Not Ready for Skill %	Total N	Total %
Domestic Living											
Housekeeping	Mild	101	63	4	3	52	33	1	1	158	100
	Moderate	88	68	3	2	37	29	1	1	129	100
	Severe	83	84	1	1	5	5	10	10	99	100
Meal preparation	Mild	120	73	4	2	33	20	8	5	165	100
	Moderate	98	73	7	5	18	14	11	8	134	100
	Severe	77	74	4	4	4	4	19	18	104	100
Shopping	Mild	104	64	5	3	45	28	8	5	162	100
	Moderate	93	69	6	5	18	14	16	12	133	100
	Severe	56	53	3	3	1	1	45	43	105	100
Money management	Mild	119	71	16	10	25	15	7	4	167	100
	Moderate	86	64	12	9	9	7	27	20	134	100
	Severe	45	43	4	4	2	2	54	51	105	100
Use of Community Resources											
Travel mobility	Mild	86	52	6	4	63	38	10	6	165	100
	Moderate	74	55	15	11	26	20	19	14	134	100
	Severe	47	45	5	5	11	11	41	39	104	100
Using the telephone	Mild	67	43	7	4	76	49	7	4	157	100
	Moderate	61	47	12	9	28	22	28	22	129	100
	Severe	38	36	7	7	7	7	52	50	104	100
Coping with emergencies	Mild	79	48	21	13	42	26	21	13	163	100
	Moderate	62	47	15	12	17	13	36	28	130	100
	Severe	37	35	11	10	3	3	56	52	107	100
Using community agencies	Mild	50	31	13	8	33	20	67	41	163	100
	Moderate	31	25	12	9	17	13	68	53	128	100
	Severe	14	14	6	6	1	1	81	79	102	100
Behavior Management											
Interpersonal relationships	Mild	127	77	9	5	26	16	3	2	165	100
	Moderate	101	75	6	5	23	17	4	3	134	100
	Severe	86	81	3	3	8	8	9	8	106	100
Behavior control	Mild	109	66	5	3	49	30	2	1	165	100
	Moderate	98	75	2	2	28	21	3	2	131	100
	Severe	84	80	4	4	10	10	6	6	104	100
Social and recreational activities	Mild	117	71	8	5	38	23	2	1	165	100
	Moderate	106	80	5	4	19	14	2	2	132	100
	Severe	95	90	3	3	1	1	6	6	105	100

Appendix G

Additional Data On Study Group Members Who Returned to the Institution Versus Those Who Remained in the Community

TABLE G.1
LEVEL OF RETARDATION AMONG THOSE WHO RETURNED
AND THOSE WHO REMAINED

Study Group	Level of Retardation							
	Mild		Moderate		Severe		Total	
	N	%	N	%	N	%	N	%
Returned	22	42	23	43	8	15	53	100
Remained	155	41	118	31	81	26	374	100

TABLE G.2
AGE OF THOSE WHO RETURNED AND THOSE WHO REMAINED

Study Group	Children		Adults		Total	
	N	%	N	%	N	%
Returned	8	15	45	85	53	100
Remained	45	20	285	80	330	100

TABLE G.3
UTILIZATION OF AND NEED FOR SERVICES
AMONG THOSE WHO RETURNED AND THOSE WHO REMAINED

Type of Service	Used Returned N	Used Returned %	Used Remained N	Used Remained %	Needed, Not Used Returned N	Needed, Not Used Returned %	Needed, Not Used Remained N	Needed, Not Used Remained %	Not Needed, Not Used Returned N	Not Needed, Not Used Returned %	Not Needed, Not Used Remained N	Not Needed, Not Used Remained %
Health Care Needs		37		54		9		8		50		35
Medical Services	42	72	360	94	1	2	4	1	12	21	15	4
Dental	32	55	301	79	5	9	32	8	18	31	—	—
Physical Therapy	3	5	40	11	3	5	23	6	49	85	318	83
Speech Therapy	8	14	118	31	11	19	61	16	36	62	201	53
Social and Recreational Needs		44		53		19		8		35		36
Recreational/social activities	36	62	318	83	14	24	23	5	6	11	39	11
Social and psychological therapy	36	62	215	56	10	17	26	7	10	17	130	36
Camp programs	14	24	146	38	10	18	38	10	30	52	137	36
Occupational therapy	15	26	125	33	9	15	29	8	34	59	227	59
Other Needs		19		29		7		3		69		68
Employment placement	22	38	196	52	9	16	15	4	24	41	165	43
Housing assistance	6	10	96	25	1	2	9	2	47	81	275	73
Legal assistance	5	9	36	9	1	2	7	2	49	84	335	88
Average		34		46		12		6		49		44

TABLE G.4
UTILIZATION OF AND NEED FOR TRAINING
AMONG THOSE WHO RETURNED AND THOSE WHO REMAINED

Type of Training	Received				Needed, Not Received				Not Needed, Not Received							
									Already Had Skill				Not Ready for Skill			
	Returned		Remained		Returned		Remained		Returned		Remained		Returned		Remained	
	N	%	N	%	N	%	N	%	N	%	N	%	N	%	N	%
Personal Maintenance		35		39		1		1		54		40		1		5
Eating	31	53	174	46	1	2	3	1	21	36	126	33	—	—	2	<1
Toileting	6	10	56	15	—	—	3	1	44	76	235	62	1	2	4	1
Dressing	10	17	85	22	1	2	3	1	41	71	211	55	—	—	4	1
Cleanliness	30	52	205	54	—	—	2	<1	23	40	101	27	—	—	70	18
Grooming	25	43	213	56	—	—	3	1	26	45	90	24	2	3	7	3
Sensory Development		19		33		5		5		67		55		1		1
Motor	8	14	117	31	1	2	17	5	45	77	227	59	1	2	1	<1
Hearing and vision	4	7	72	19	1	2	7	2	49	84	277	73	—	—	2	<1
Speech and language	21	36	191	50	6	10	33	9	24	41	129	34	1	2	4	1
Education and Employment		36		55		12		5		24		22		14		12
Preacademic	16	28	165	43	2	3	9	2	30	52	174	46	2	3	6	2
Numbers and telling time	21	36	222	58	5	9	24	6	15	26	80	21	9	15	—	—
Reading and writing	20	34	225	59	8	14	32	8	9	16	55	14	10	17	57	15
Prevocational	30	52	241	63	6	10	8	2	10	18	65	17	6	10	53	14
Vocational	18	31	196	51	13	22	21	6	5	9	39	10	15	26	110	29
Domestic Living		53		66		10		3		14		16		16		13
Housekeeping	32	55	255	67	6	10	4	1	11	19	91	24	1	2	13	3
Meal preparation	32	55	280	73	6	10	10	3	7	12	54	14	9	16	31	8
Shopping	27	47	239	62	6	10	10	2	9	16	58	15	13	22	65	17
Money management	31	53	232	61	6	11	28	7	4	7	34	9	14	24	84	22
Use of Community Resources		23		41		15		7		23		20		31		30
Travel and mobility	20	34	197	52	5	9	23	6	16	28	90	24	13	22	66	17
Using the telephone	12	22	161	42	7	12	20	5	21	36	100	26	12	21	84	22
Coping with emergencies	14	24	175	46	13	23	36	9	10	17	57	15	18	31	104	27
Using community agencies	7	12	89	23	10	17	28	7	5	9	49	13	28	48	204	54
Behavior Management		68		76		13		2		7		18		6		2
Interpersonal relationships	40	69	294	77	9	15	11	3	3	5	58	15	3	5	13	3
Behavior management	43	74	267	70	4	7	7	2	6	10	88	23	1	2	10	3
Social and recreational activities	35	60	305	80	10	17	7	2	4	7	57	15	6	11	4	1
Average		38		51		9		4		32		28		12		11

Index